A SOLDIER'S DIARY

P6 73

VANWELL
VOICES
of WAR

DONALD STUART MACPHERSON

A SOLDIER'S DIARY

THE WWI DIARIES OF DONALD MACPHERSON

Vanwell Publishing Limited

St. Catharines, Ontario

Vanwell Publishing acknowledges the financial support of the Government of Canada through the Book Publishing Industry Development Program for our publishing activities.

Design: Linda Moroz-Irvine

Vanwell Publishing Limited
1 Northrup Crescent
P.O. Box 2131
St. Catharines, Ontario L2R 7S2

Printed in Canada

Canadian Cataloguing in Publication Data

Macpherson, Donald Stuart, 1895-1991
          A soldier's diary : the WWI diaries of Donald Macpherson

(Vanwell voices of war)
ISBN 1-55125-068-3
ISSN 1498-8844

  1. Macpherson, Donald Stuart, 1895-1991–Diaries. 2. World
War, 1914-1918–Personal narratives, Canadian. 3. Canada.
Canadian Army. Battery, 9ᵗʰ–Biography. I. Title. II. Series.

D640.M29 2001   940.4'8171   C2001-902011-2

FOREWORD

My father, Donald Stuart Macpherson, was born in Orangeville Ontario, one of six sons of Dugald and Sarah Macpherson, on 17 March 1895. The First World War broke out while he was a student at the Faculty of Education, University of Toronto and at the same time in training with the C.O.T.C. In July 1916 he enlisted as gunner in the 67th (Varsity) Battery, which moved to Niagara-on-the-Lake and then to Petawawa.

Mr. Macpherson left Petawawa with the Battery's fourth draft for Halifax, arriving aboard S.S. *Grampian* in Liverpool on 26 October. He was assigned to a signalling course at Shorncliffe Camp, near Folkestone, and on 19 January 1917 sailed from Southampton for France. Assigned to the 9th Battery C.F.A., he was to be present at the great battles of Vimy Ridge, Hill 70 and Passchendaele, earning a Military Medal at the latter.

In December he returned to England for a cadet course and was then commissioned as a lieutenant in May 1918. Returning to France, he was posted to the 23rd Battery and, on 8 August 1918, was wounded at the Battle of Amiens. He spent the remainder of the war convalescing at several military hospitals before sailing for home on 2 February 1919 in the hospital ship *Araguaya*.

Demobilized in March 1919, Mr. Macpherson taught at Annette Street school in Toronto until 1929, during this period attending summer courses at Queen's University, Kingston, graduating in 1929. He was subsequently principal of a succession of seven Toronto public schools, retiring in 1960. He died at Port Hope in 1991.

His five small diaries comprise an engagingly articulate account of his wartime experiences. A most striking feature is the way in which he was able to make contact with his brothers, officers in three different units: Douglas in the 16th Canadian Scottish Regiment, Ewart in the Royal Flying Corps, and Ross in Princess Patricia's Canadian Light Infantry. All four were together in London on New Year's Day, 1918. Only Ross did not survive the war, and was killed on 26 August 1918. It is worth noting that Ewart served in an administrative role with the RCAF during the Second World War, while the youngest of the six Macpherson brothers, Arthur, also served in the RCAF as a chaplain.

Ken Macpherson
Port Hope
January 2001

Dear Family:

My War Diary has remained almost unopened for nearly fifty years. It is quite an experience to open it now and read the thoughts and impressions of the person I was in those far-off heroic and sacrificial days of World War I. Much of it is of interest only to myself and would seem tedious and inconsequential to any other reader. But some parts of it you may wish to read. It doesn't say much about the strategy and tactics of modern warfare; but it may tell you something of the way in which a whole generation of Canadians responded to the call of duty, heedless of the cost and conscious only of the privilege of serving their country and the cause of world freedom.

600,000 Canadians took part in this conflict; 60,000 did not come back.

> "They are too near to be great,
> But our children shall understand
> When and how our fate was changed
> And by whose hand."

Dad.

Jan. 24, 1965.

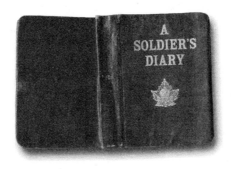

MY WAR DIARY
1916 — 1919

MARCH 17 – JULY 14, 1916 ENLISTMENT

March 17, 1916 Having finished up my work at Annette Street School for the week now ending, I very fittingly celebrated my coming of age by journeying (through zero weather at 11:00 p.m.) to St. Michael's Hospital, there to undergo an operation to fit me for active service with the Canadian forces overseas.

March 18, 1916 Operation successfully performed at 8:00 a.m. by Drs. Silverthorn and Graham. Three weeks' residence in hospital are now in prospect. With careful handling I should be in the army at last by next midsummer.

March 24, *1916*   Many happy returns of this day to brother Ross! May I soon be over with him to take my share of the hardships and dangers that he has been undergoing.

April 8, *1916*   Obtained my release from the hospital this afternoon. Was driven by George Garton to 103 Macdonnell Ave. (the Creeds'), where I am to spend a week of convalescence during which I hope to recover my powers of locomotion. Three weeks nearer enlistment!

April 17, *1916*   Back to school today after just four weeks' absence. Feel shaky yet, but the Easter vacation (April 21-30) should set me up again.

April 18, *1916*   Ewart's birthday today! Best wishes to No. 3 soldier brother from his would-be No. 4 ditto. I hope I may prove as efficient a soldier as he has shown himself to be. It would be a joke if I were to beat him to France after all!

April 30, *1916*   This day I celebrate the birthday of one whom all the deep affection and sincere respect of his six sons cannot repay for his labour and worry of many years in our behalf. Father o' mine, it has been hard to show the love we do feel for you in spite of thoughtless deeds and words that may have caused you to think us unappreciative. This page is dedicated to you because my love is greater than can be expressed in spoken words—and is indeed imperfectly written down here. May we have more happy years together.

June 8, *1916*   The Toronto Board of Education at its meeting tonight granted me leave of absence, with salary privileges, to take effect at the close of the present term. How wonderfully the way has been opened for me towards the final realization of my desire to enlist! What seemed an idle dream a year ago will soon be an accomplished fact.

June 21, 1916   The greatest of all women celebrates her birthday today: my mother! No words can ever express her worth; no human mind can ever quite conceive of so noble a nature, so steadfast a purpose to influence the world for good. We, her sons, can only worship her with silent reverence and seek by our imperfect lives to merit a part of the great love she bears us. We can never repay her; but pray God we shall strive always to live in accordance with her magnificent ideals. May God grant her many more years of life and us the privilege, the happiness and joy that should be hers after long years of patient labour in our behalf.

My entry for June 21st would indeed be incomplete without an acknowledgment of my unbounded pride in brother Doug, whose birthday also is today. In far-off France he fights for king and country with the splendid courage and perseverance so characteristic of him. In all the dangers and hardships through which he is passing may no evil befall him; and when this cloud of warfare passes may he return safe and sound to those to whom he is very dear.

June 29, 1916   My year at Annette Street School ended at noon today. When shall I be able to return to the duties that have been so pleasant though strenuous? It is hard, at the last moment, to bid farewell to all the associations with teachers and pupils that have been so enjoyable. But such considerations must indeed be forgotten when the big duty calls.

July 13, 1916   Entrance reports today convey news of the success of ten of my Junior 4 pupils. A very gratifying result!

July 14, 1916   After nearly two years of impatient waiting I am at last a full-fledged member of the Canadian Expeditionary Force. I took the oath this morning and have been attested to the 67th (Varsity) Battery, Canadian Field Artillery. By reason of Angus's expected arrival I have obtained leave of absence until July 24. Ross and Doug are both now in France and Ewart is at Camp Borden. The family has now its largest possible representation with the colours.

July 24, 1916   Reported for duty today at the headquarters of the Varsity Battery. Entire equipment not immediately available, but I have the supreme satisfaction of being at last in active training for service with the C.E.F.

July 26, 1916   Paraded today in uniform. The Battery, as expected, comprises many very fine fellows who will make quite pleasant company while we are together. Angus left for the West this morning after a very short visit. I spent the night with him at 93 Rose Avenue (George Garton's).

August 4, 1916   Today has witnessed our transfer to Camp Niagara, on orders received only Wednesday evening. It is a change for the better, as our training in Toronto was not of a very comprehensive nature. We are not yet equipped with horses or guns.

AUGUST 6-25, 1916 CAMP NIAGARA

August 6, 1916   Today I have had the leisure to renew acquaintance with the familiar landmarks in and about this old campground. Memory brings back the experience of other years, when I was but a make-believe soldier [with the C.O.T.C. at the University of Toronto]. Freshest in my mind, because it was only fifteen short months ago, is the recollection of the two short weeks spent here with Ross while he was on his way through with the First Universities Company. Already he has had a year's experience of the danger and hardships of war. If my going could but relieve him of the need for further service, my cup of happiness would indeed be full. May I soon be privileged at least to share with him the stress and strain of this conflict.

August 12, 1916   With some difficulty I secured leave to come home over the weekend to bid goodbye to Ewart and Young Doug, and Kate Thomson, who are starting for the West on Sunday. I dread the added loneliness their departure will bring to the folks at home. I am obliged to return to camp by Monday morning's train and boat. Left Niagara this morning at 11 a.m., reaching home by the regular evening train.

August 14, 1916   Reached camp again at 4:30 p.m. My visit home, though short, was a very happy one. I am hoping for at least one more leave before we are moved farther away. There is a possibility of our being transferred to Petawawa before long.

August 22, 1916   Today Percy Avison reported for duty with the 67th Battery. It will be a pleasure to have him with me, though my sympathy goes out to Aunt Annie and Uncle John and Fidella in the anxiety that will be theirs. Rumours persist that we are soon to go to Petawawa. It will be a long way from home, but undoubtedly our training will be improved with the better equipment that awaits us there. Here our work has been one long succession of "fatigue" with very little practical instruction in artillery.

August 25, 1916   At 6:30 this evening we entrained for Petawawa with the 69th, 70th, and 71st Batteries. Our route took us through Niagara Falls and we caught a fleeting glimpse of the "Horseshoe" as we passed. At Hamilton a half-hour stop was made, and reaching North Toronto at 11:30, we were given a cheer by the considerable crowd of people gathered there. But ere long we had left all familiar scenes behind us and were speeding through the darkness of night towards our wilderness home.

August 26, 1916   Woke up at 5 a.m., just in time to catch a glimpse of Trenton as we passed through. A long wait at Smith's Falls and then a quick run up the beautiful Ottawa valley through Renfrew and Pembroke to this famous artillery camp, Petawawa. First impressions were rendered some-what unfavourable by a heavy downfall of rain, but before evening we were comfortably settled in the lines recently vacated by the 12th Brigade.

AUGUST 26-OCTOBER 21 CAMP PETAWAWA

August 27, 1916   Reveille at 6:30 this morning wakened us to the glory of a beautiful Sunday morning. From the ridge of land just beyond our lines we have a magnificent view of the Ottawa valley, both banks heavily wooded with evergreen. The river widens out to a considerable lake and the land rises by easy stages until, far in the distance, the Laurentians raise their heads into the low-lying clouds. Ever-changing shades of blue haze clothe the more distant heights with a splendour that is indescribable. In spite of the warlike nature of our closer surroundings war seems very unreal and far away in this "home of nature."

August 28, 1916   Our real artillery training has at last begun. We have sixty horses and four 12-pdr guns, and our time from Reveille at 5:15 a.m. to Lights Out at 10:15 p.m. will be well filled with work. My first ride today was quite an interesting experience, but I cannot vouch for the gracefulness of my appearance on horseback. It is quite evident to us all that we have much to learn before we shall be ready to "strafe" the Huns.

August 29, 1916   I have been called upon with nine others to take the course in Signalling. It promises interesting work but I am very sorry to miss practice on the guns. I am particularly fortunate in the men with whom I am living in the tent:

Cpl. Fydell, Bdr. Vallentyne, Driver Percy Avison, and Gunners Hoover, Duke and Begg—what better comrades in arms could I wish for!

August 30, 1916   Have discovered that Lad. Stevenson is in camp with the 56th Bty. It is to leave for overseas shortly, however. Today I met Kilty, King and White of the Faculty of Education course, 1914-15. They are with the 50th Bty, 13th Bde. It is a pleasure to meet all these old acquaintances.

September 2, 1916   We had our first long ride today. Three hours in the saddle has left many of us tired and sore but wealthier in experience.

September 6, 1916   Four Orangeville boys reported here for duty today: Harry Firth, Stuart Porter, Bill Henderson, and Alex Fleming. They seem very young for soldiering but will doubtless make good with the Battery. Percy Avison is gaining the reputation of being one of the best drivers in the Battery. He has taken very kindly to the work and proves a cheerful companion under all circumstances. The time for reveille has been advanced to 6 a.m.—a more reasonable time in view of the present schedule of Mr. Morning Sun.

September 13, 1916   Douglas Macpherson Jr. is just a year old today. He is certainly a fine, sturdy little youngster and has surely a great future before him. What a depth of affection a baby can arouse in one's heart! May he be blessed with every opportunity and every influence that will make him truly great.

September 22, 1916   Arthur's birthday anniversary today richly deserves mention here. Seldom will be witnessed a more thorough and uncomplaining application to the commonplace duties at home than the youngest of us is showing. It is a comfort to us who must needs go out and fight for a good cause to know that the folks at home will be well looked after. Here I must record my deepest gratitude to the Great Ruler of the Universe for such parents and such brothers as are mine. It is a blessing for which my best endeavours can never make return but which will never fail to stimulate me to the highest things to which I can aspire.

September 23, 1916   Four weeks of our stay here have passed quickly away. Two more weeks might witness our departure. The longer one stays at Petawawa the more one appreciates the beauties of its surroundings and the splendid opportunities it offers for efficient artillery training. It will be a pleasure always to look back on this part of my soldiering career.

September 29, 1916   This morning the announcement was suddenly made that a draft of fifteen men from the 67th must leave for overseas tomorrow. Nothing can picture the consternation of all in this Battery, for it means no last leave for those who are to go. To my sincere sorrow three of the Orangeville boys are named for the draft, though they have been with the Battery only three weeks. All my efforts have failed to release Bill Henderson, Harry Firth, and Alex Fleming from so sudden a departure. Three times I volunteered to go in place of one or other of them, for I am more ready to go than they, but each time I was refused. I have done my utmost to outfit them properly for the journey, but I feel sorry for them and for their folks at home, who cannot see them to bid them goodbye. They are game youngsters and I hope to join them "over there" before long.

October 1, 1916   Last night and today the camp has been again stirred by the report that a large draft from each Battery will leave for England about the third week of this month. The 67th Battery is to send two officers and ninety-six men, so nearly all of us will certainly be called upon to go. Four days' leave will doubtless be given us, but I dread my visit home for the sorrow my departure will bring this time to my parents. When will this brutal war cease, so that we may all return to bring relief from the anxiety to those who are dear to us! It is a privilege to be given the strength to do one's duty, but it is a thousand times harder when it is others who must bear the greater sorrow.

October 2, 1916   My signalling course progresses favourably and I begin to hope of securing my certificate before we leave. Signaller Fleming went away on the draft on Saturday, so the class now numbers only nine: McCamus, Shaver, Ketchum, Drybrough, Pinnock, Burton, Eakins, Smith, and myself. Tonight I had my first inoculation, also a vaccination. The after-effects are rather unpleasant but I'm glad to have it over with.

October 4, 1916   The list of the men detailed for the coming overseas draft was posted today. As expected, I am on it as are practically all my close friends in the Battery, except Val (who is to be the Q.M.S.), Percy (his assistant) and Mel (who intends taking the course at Kingston). Within a month or less we shall be on the "briny deep."

October 5, 1916   Leave has been arranged for half the Battery from Friday night to Wednesday reveille. I have wired home tonight to prepare the folks for my arrival Saturday morning. I hope Ewart will get home, for otherwise I shall not see him before leaving for England. It will be a hasty visit, with the sadness of leave-taking at the end of it; but I shall be glad to see all the people and the familiar scenes in Orangeville and Toronto once again before embarking on this uncertain enterprise across the seas.

October 7, 1916   Home again and everybody well. Leaving Petawawa at 7:00 last evening, we arrived at Toronto Union Station by special train about 6:40 this morning. The coaches were poorly heated and sleep was next to impossible, but that was a mere detail so long as the train sped homeward. The train leaving North Toronto for Owen Sound at 8:00 a.m landed me at Orangeville at 10:00. Ewart met me at the station, having procured leave until Monday morning. I found the family comfortably settled in their new residence on Second Street.

October 8, 1916   Church twice, hurried visits to various Orangeville friends, and pleasant little chats with the home folks filled up my first whole day here. Surely the memory of this day will stay with me, whatever long weary months may intervene before I return again. Mother is marvellously brave about the future, but I dread for her sake the sorrow of Tuesday morning's leavetaking.

October 9, 1916   Five days ago I little expected to spend Thanksgiving Day at home; so I have this unexpected pleasure, among so many other things to be thankful for. I have managed to finish up my visiting and have now the leisure to "hang around" the house, as oft before, chatting with Mother and getting in her way at every turn. She is always busy, this little mother o' mine; maybe that's how she overcomes the sorrows and anxieties that might otherwise overcome her.

October 10, 1916   Left home this morning on my return journey to Petawawa. Thank God for such parents! They were wonderfully calm and brave as I bade them goodbye at the station, else my own feelings might have overcome me. Surely the good Lord will not for too long withhold us all from coming back to those so dear to us and to whom we are so dear. In Toronto I had the pleasure of seeing sister Marjorie [Marjorie Richardson, Ross's fiancee] and accompanying her as far as West Toronto Station on her way back to Guelph. I spent a very enjoyable hour at old Annette bidding goodbye to teachers and pupils. The Creeds and Gartons, as usual, did all they could to cheer me on my way. George and family, with Will and Carolyn, saw me off at the station, where a large crowd had assembled to witness our departure. Leaving at 8:00, we journeyed comfortably all night, arriving back at camp at seven in the morning.

October 11, 1916   Now that our leave is over, we are all anxious to get away from here at an early date. We hear that we may go on the 21st, which is not too soon in view of the cold weather now prevailing here. I received my second inoculation this afternoon, without any serious after-effects except the usual soreness in the chest and arm. My vaccination of a week ago Monday has bothered me very little thus far. John Garton presented me with a very good air pillow on my way through Toronto yesterday. It is a very useful gift and folds into quite a small space.

October 14, 1916   A postcard received from Mother tonight conveys the news that Doug has been wounded, but not seriously. It is a relief to be assured that there is no need for worry about him.

October 15, 1916   A list was posted up today with the names of sixty men of the 67th Battery who are to leave for overseas about next Saturday. It is understood that the remainder of the ninety-six men listed on October 4th will follow in a week's time. The first draft includes nearly all the older men of the Battery, most of them Varsity men. I could wish for no better comrades in my journey across the Atlantic and my subsequent training in England. Was unable to have Stuart Porter included in this first lot.

October 18, 1916   Today I was given by Capt. Johnston the choice of going back to Toronto with the Battery for the winter or staying on the draft. My choice could not be other than to stay with the draft, though I well realized the relief it would give the home folk if I were to stay. Third (and last) inoculation this afternoon. After-effects quite mild.

October 20, 1916   Yesterday and today we have been taking tests in Signalling. While the results will not reach us for some time, I have good reason to believe that I succeeded in obtaining Grade A standing. We have been granted permission to wear the crossed flags. I am now nearly ready for overseas. We leave tomorrow.

OCTOBER 21-24, 1916
PETAWAWA TO HALIFAX FOR OVERSEAS

October 21, 1916   We have had most of the day to ourselves in order to prepare for our long journey. I purchased six English pounds and wired home to tell them of my departure. Our train with 500 artillerymen aboard pulled out from the camp siding at 7:00 this evening. Val and Percy helped us to the station with our kits and each handed us a box of "eats" to add to the comfort of our journey. They have both been very generous in helping us prepare for the trip. At Pembroke we were very heartily greeted and showered with eats; I was speaking to Gordon Hayes, Harold Kilpatrick and Velma Youmans for a few minutes. We reached Smith's Falls at midnight and, after an hour's stop, sped onward into the night towards Montreal.

October 22, 1916   I wakened up about six this morning, just as we were entering Montreal. Stopped for an hour on the outskirts of the city. Mount Royal, Notre Dame Cathedral and other places of interest could be seen in the distance. Travelling now over the I.C.R. we crossed over Victoria Bridge and journeyed on with few stops through Ste. Hyacinthe and Drummondville. The landscape is typically French-Canadian, with long narrow farms and frame whitewashed buildings all along the way on either side. At Chaudière a lengthy stop was made (2:30 p.m.) and we went out through the town on a route march. A large stone church is the central feature; nothing else of special interest. Leaving Chaudière, we had a splendid though distant view of the famous Quebec Bridge. We were disappointed not to see Quebec City; our train did not take the loop through Lévis. The Chaudière River and the falls made a very pretty picture as we passed in the twilight. A few miles farther on the St. Lawrence came into view once more with the Laurentians standing out in the gloom beyond. A stop was made at Rivière du Loup and a song service was held in our honour under YMCA direction.

October 23, 1916   I was asleep when we passed through Rimouski and did not waken until we had left Quebec Province and entered New Brunswick at Campbellton about 7 a.m. Here we had to change our time one hour as were entering the

Atlantic Time Zone. From a short distance past Campbellton right on to Bathurst we were almost continuously within sight of Chaleur Bay: narrow at first but finally widening out beyond our sight. Newcastle, our next stop, is beautifully located on the Miramichi River; it has a fine wireless station and seems to be quite a stirring town. Thus far in N.B. our course had taken us through endless miles of bush and over countless rivers and streams. From Newcastle on there is considerable farming land on either side. We came to Moncton about 4 p.m. and turned out again for a route march through this city of about 15,000 people. Then over another provincial boundary we sped, reaching Amherst, N.S., at 8 p.m. for a short stop only. Detention camp visible from the train.

October 24, 1916 We slept during the rest of our train journey and wakened at 6 o'clock this Tuesday morning in Halifax station. Posted a card by kindness of a passer-by, ate a substantial breakfast, packed up kits and blankets and waited for orders. We marched to the wharf about 10:30 a.m. and boarded H.M.T. *Grampian* (Allan Line) where we are comfortably quartered in 2nd class compartments. Six in our cabin: Hoover, Dickson, Mooney, Glover, Mason and self. Of the city we can see little except the Citadel and the Harbour surroundings. I got a letter off to Mother, to be mailed after the ship sails. There are about 1000 troops aboard, including the 203rd Bn from Winnipeg, a C.A.M.C. detachment and artillerymen. Fruit vendors are thriving on our surplus wealth.

OCTOBER 25-NOVEMBER 5, 1916
HALIFAX TO LIVERPOOL

October 25, 1916   A hot bath, a sound sleep and a wakening to a
beautiful day: all these help to put one in good spirits. Just
as I wakened at 6:30 the ship moved away from the dock
and anchored out in the harbour. The *Mauretania* passed us
inward bound. We are to go over together. Two cruisers and
a destroyer are nearby, so we are given assurance of safety.
The meals are quite good and everything points to a comfortable and interesting voyage, but no one knows when we
are to start. This afternoon the *Empress of Britain* cast anchor
beside us.

October 26, 1916   Today we have come under the regular routine
of duties which is to govern us during the voyage: reveille
at 6:30, breakfast at 7:00 (first sitting), parade 9 to 11:30,
dinner 11:45, parade 2 to 4 p.m., supper at 5:00, last post
9:15, lights out at 9:30. I am sleeping splendidly, eating well
and finding everything very interesting. Today is dull and
blustery with rain. We learn that the Corsican is in harbour;
probably we are to wait until the four transport ships can
go together with adequate escort for all.

At 4:45 our good ship drew up anchor, sailed out of
Bedford Basin past the wharves of the city, past the strongly fortified island at the mouth of the harbour, through the
gap in the steel boom that connects it with the mainland and
out into the open sea. H.M.T *Corsican* is following us and a
cruiser is in the lead. At about 6 o'clock we bade goodbye
to the last bit of land fading away behind us in the gloom.

How many long months will pass before we greet this same bit of our homeland on our return?

October 27, 1916   First day out and no enemy yet in sight! We are following a zigzag course, with the *Corsican* now ahead of us and *Grampian* bringing up the rear. The sea is not rough, but even a normal swell has been sufficient to cause considerable sickness among the troops on board. So far I have escaped, beyond a few uncertain moments last night and again this morning. An interesting diversion was caused by a school of porpoises that passed on our port side. This afternoon a large ship (Dutch) passed us, inward bound. We are not making much speed and shall probably have a lengthy voyage. Many of our draft (myself included) have been warned for guard duty tomorrow.

October 28, 1916   At 8 o'clock this morning we commenced what was to prove a very wearisome 24 hours' guard duty. Early in the day we ran into a nor'easter gale, with persistent rain during my two-hour shift on the saloon deck. The afternoon, however, with the sun on the job again proved quite enjoyable. We were not allowed to go back to our own bunks between shifts during the night and could not sleep at all because of over-crowding in the guardroom. One of my night shifts was unpleasantly spent in the steerage. I pity the unfortunate troops who have to live down there during the entire voyage.

October 29, 1916   According to information vouchsafed by a deckhand we cleared Newfoundland last night. All morning we have been sailing north, but now we are heading east once more. The wind has veered to westward and is very strong. The sea in consequence has become rough, with waves coming in over the decks. It is a magnificent sight, this stormy ocean: ponderous, slow-moving but all-conquering billows, green and blue, rising and breaking far upwards in a crest of white foam. The vessel rolls heavily under the buffeting it is receiving. What an insignificant thing is the work of man when faced with the tremendous might of nature! And yet, we sail steadily forward, guided in safety by the same omnipotent Hand that controls the raging deep. I think it was this thought that imparted a feeling of awe to all who attended the church service this morning in the Second Class dining hall as we did reverence to the Maker of all things, great and small.

October 30, 1916   With a heavy sea still running and a goodly number of men and officers on the sick list, no parade was held today. One advantage of a high sea is the immunity it gives from submarine attack; but having sailed some 1100 miles we should soon be out of the danger zone anyway. We all wear life belts continuously when out of our cabins. Today we passed the *Calgarian* or the *Metagama*; the opinions of our informers vary. We learn that our escort is the cruiser *Antrim* of North Sea fame, also that one of the cruisers with us at Halifax was the *Leviathan* and the other the converted cruiser *Sydney*. Writing is almost impossible because of the motion of the vessel. I am feeling O.K.

though my appetite is not up to the mark. We hope to land either Saturday or Sunday next.

October 31, 1916   The wind still keeps the sea running high, but the weather today has been bright and fair and the air is most invigorating. We have on board distinguished passengers in the persons of Sir Hemar and Lady Greenwood. Their children, Haswell and Sheila, have made many friends among the soldiers on board. Tonight the artillery draft gave a concert in the Second Class dining saloon. I had the pleasure of participating as a member of the Varsity Battery Sextet. Halloween was celebrated later on by some of the men, to the discomfiture of others.

November 1, 1916   A day of steady progress, devoid of any noteworthy incident. We passed the *Scandinavian* at long range. It is quite remarkable at night to watch the phosphorescent lights that shine mysteriously out of the briny depths where the water has been stirred up by the passage of our ship. Even out in the darkness on either side, where the waves break ceaselessly against each other, these strange lights appear and disappear as if operated by a secret system of illumination down below. Each day we are able to learn about outstanding events in various parts of the world, particularly in the war zones, by reading the Marconigram bulletin posted by the ship's officers.

November 2, 1916   "General alarms" are the order of the day as we near the danger zone around the British Isles. Two or three times a day the alarm sounds and we have practice in assembling on deck in the shortest possible time. Tonight the sergeants gave a concert, at the close of which a few N.C.O.s and men were asked to provide some music for passengers in the First Class saloon. Our Sextet was included and we spent quite an enjoyable time, during which we could almost imagine ourselves in somebody's drawing room back on terra firma instead of still tossing on the boundless deep. The vocal and instrumental numbers rendered by Percy McLean were especially well received. He is certainly a talented musician.

November 3, 1916   A heavy storm with wind and rain and sleet struck us this morning and all day long our vessel swayed and plunged and rolled through the tossing sea. Until afternoon I weathered the gale in good style; but a two-hour shift on guard duty in bottom steerage proved my undoing and the demon of seasickness held full sway. The return to my cabin and a few hours' sleep fixed me up all right. We are now nearing land and all are peering eagerly ahead for the first sight of shore.

November 4, 1916   Land ahoy! We passed Tory Island early this morning and presently the Emerald Isle itself appeared in the distance. Before very long we were steaming, at full speed now, along the north coast of Ireland. The sea had gradually subsided and the bright sun coloured the water a beautiful green. Our course lay through Rathlin Sound where we came within two or three miles of the Irish coast. On our port side, in the distance, Scotland loomed forth: Kintyre itself, with the Firth of Clyde beyond it leading up towards Glasgow. A few miles farther south we could distinguish to starboard the entrance to Belfast Harbour. Near at hand and all about us trawlers were searching the waters; we learned later that we were then passing the place where a collision had occurred in Friday's storm, in which a mail steamer (and 300 people) had gone down. As night came, we passed the Isle of Man and proceeded up the Mersey River towards our destination.

November 5, 1916 An early call this morning awoke us to the fact that we were resting quietly at anchor in Liverpool harbour with the Corsican (169th Bn on board) near at hand. We docked at 8 o'clock and two hours later disembarked and marched directly to the train (London and North Western Ry.) waiting for us in the depot. To a Canadian an English train has an odd appearance and we could not restrain a smile, though we knew that this "toy train" was capable of carrying us at high speed to our journey's end. We were fated not to see much of Liverpool, for our way led out through an underground route, and soon we were speeding along through the quiet fields of rural England. It was not a bright day, but words cannot express the pleasure of this Sabbath Day's journey.

The green meadows with winding streams and rivers, the frequent woodlands rich in the beauty of their fall dress, the peaceful villages and homesteads nestling among the hills, the roads and canals with well-trimmed hedges marking their course: all the changing panorama within our sight on either side was a source of keenest interest and delight to every one of us. Even the railway line showed unmistakable evidences of constant efforts to make it attractive. It was as if some magic hand had moved over the land, transforming every nook and corner into a fairyland. We gazed at it all as in a dream, yet we felt no sense of strangeness. It must be that the masters of English literature had brought these scenes before us more vividly then we realized in the reading of them; for it seemed quite a familiar country and not a land that we had never seen before. Many places of considerable importance lay along our route: Crewe, Rugby, Northampton, Wolverton, etc.

At last we were in London, the metropolis of the world, and stopped for a few minutes only at Kensington Station (4:30 p.m.). Darkness had already fallen and we could see very little of the great city. As we proceeded, our train crossed the Thames and rushed onward towards our still-distant destination. It was 8:30 when we finally reached journey's end in Shorncliffe. From the station we marched through rain to Ross Barracks, where we spent the night in an empty gun shed. Alex Fleming located me and told me that Ross had been here looking for me just yesterday on his way back to France. My disappointment may be left to the imagination! I had not counted on seeing him so soon, but to miss him by so small a margin!

TRAINING AT SHORNCLIFFE

November 6, 1916 Today, after much parading about the square, our draft was finally split up among the five reserve batteries organized here. Only five of us chose Signalling, and we were immediately attached to the 4th Reserve Bty stationed at Ross Barracks. Burns, Smith, Mason, and Orr are with me, the last three being in the same hut as I. Owen Hoover is in No. 2 Bty quartered quite near us; many others I know are within easy distance, including Harry Firth, Bill Henderson and Bob Fratt. I sent a cable home and wrote several letters.

November 9, 1916 Our duties thus far have consisted mainly of various "fatigues" but we anticipate quite a comfortable sojourn here and it will probably be February before we shall be sent to France. Shorncliffe Camp, so far as I have seen it, is well located and well organized. It is almost exclusively Canadian and one meets many acquaintances. From the vicinity of Ross Barracks can be seen the Strait of Dover and beyond on a clear day (they say) the coast of France. Over to the east lies the town of Dover, from which at night powerful searchlights are directed upwards in search of hostile aircraft. In the daytime aeroplanes and one or two dirigibles are constantly patrolling the coast and near us a battery of anti-aircraft guns practices on an imagined enemy. We are indeed getting near the scene of action of this great war and around are signs of earnest preparation.

November 10, 1916   Wednesday evening and again tonight I went down to Folkestone. It is a very interesting place and from The Leas one obtains a magnificent view of the Strait. Quite a cosmopolitan air is given this town of some 15,000 population by the intermingling of Canadians, Australians and New Zealanders in large numbers. The Anzac troops are members of units on their way to France. Their training in England is carried on at Salisbury Plains. We are settling down quite contentedly. The weather has been unusually fine. So far we have taken only a little semaphore drill, but we hope soon to get going properly. No mail has reached me yet, either from home or from Ross or Doug.

November 11, 1916   This afternoon again I went down to Folkestone and in the evening dined with Capt. Firth at Caves Café. Spent a very pleasant evening and walked back to camp through Sandgate. It is just a week ago that Capt. Firth was speaking to Ross for a few minutes down at West Sandling Camp, so I have had first-hand information of Ross's welfare at that time.

November 12, 1916   Paraded to church this morning and listened to an inspiring speech by Capt. W.A. Cameron, formerly of Bloor Street Baptist church, Toronto. This afternoon I walked down to Sandgate, proceeded by bus to Hythe and walked up the hill to Sandling Camp in search of Mr. Denton. I found his present location but missed seeing him.

November 13, 1916   A letter reached me today from R.B. McGuire [later accidentally killed in training], who is still in England (at Watford, Herts Co.). It was a pleasure to hear from him and I hope to see him before either of us leaves for France.

November 14, 1916   Yesterday and today I spent on kitchen fatigue. Rather an uninteresting occupation to have for two successive days! But it is all in the game and there are no complaints coming, although this delay in getting down to real business is more than a little irksome. In the evening I had the pleasure of dining with Mrs. (Col.) Preston and Eileen at their temporary home in Folkestone, 11 Bouverie Square. Brown (brother-in-law of Rev. Mr. Howitt, Orangeville) was with me and we certainly spent a most delightful evening. Ross had visited Mrs. Preston on November 4th, just before leaving for France, so I again had news of him from friends who had recently seen him. I also learned for sure that Doug has been only slightly wounded, but my information ended there. Surely word will soon come from France, for it is a week ago that I wrote.

November 15, 1916   This morning I was detailed with fifteen others from the 4th Bty to take the course in riding. So suddenly I have become so busy that I have hardly time to eat my meals. The riding is very severe and tiring else it would be much more enjoyable. Tonight I am sore indeed and so stiff that I shall hardly be able to sleep. It will be a relief to have this part of my training over! No mail yet.

November 17, 1916   A letter each from my mother, Ross, Mr. Biggart, and a card from Mr. Adams received today. A telegram from Doug arrived at noon from London asking me to meet him there Sunday. Replied this (Friday) evening, having obtained permission for leave over the weekend from the Riding School.

November 18, 1916   Left for London on the 12:41 train, arriving Charing Cross Stn. about 3:30 p.m. Found my wire, undelivered, at the Charles St. Branch of the Maple Leaf Club. I found that Doug had gone to Hants Co. last evening. Wired to his address there and spent the night at the club.

November 19, 1916   A wire from Doug received about 11 o'clock this morning, announces his return to London today. Went over to see Barbara Macpherson [sister of John Macpherson] in the afternoon and Doug arrived there about 7:30. We had a very happy visit together until the time I had to leave (9:15 train from Charing Cross). Sent a cable home. Arrived back at camp about midnight. Doug is going up to Scotland but hopes to come down to Shorncliffe at the end of this week.

November 20, 1916   Back to the ride again, with weather wet and muddy. Lots of mail. Three letters and four cards from mother and two letters from Angus. Letter from John Macpherson.

November 24, 1916   Passed out of the riding course this morning, but detailed for "stables" over the weekend. Spent the evening with Doug, who arrived this afternoon.

November 25, 1916   Cleaning harness till noon. Afternoon and evening with Doug. Met Capt. and Harry Firth and Charlie Morrison. Doug went to see Jim Thomson. We visited Mrs. Preston at night.

November 26, 1916   Saw Doug off by the 10:10 train for London. His leave expires at midnight. Still on stables. Met Harold Bedford.

November 29, 1916   Letter from Doug. This seems to be a week of drill and fatigues. Attached to "A" recruit squad for Signalling instruction.

November 30, 1916   A new draft arrived tonight at Ross Barracks: probably the one expected from Petawawa. A letter from Mother; disappointed to find it older than the last one received.

December 1, 1916   Alan Cameron and Stuart Porter are both in camp with the latest draft from Canada; some thirty 67th chaps in all, with Capt. Johnston in command.

December 2, 1916   On town picket in Folkestone: a wearisome task, parading at 4 p.m. and on duty till 11:00. An object lesson on the evils of drink, a serious problem among the troops here in England.

December 3, 1916   Church parade and a lazy afternoon. Service at Y.M.C.A. at night.

December 4 to 9, 1916   On signal course with "B" Recruit Squad. First mail from home direct to my present address, including generous parcels from various friends.

December 11 to 16, 1916   Posted to No. 1 squad with 100%. Another full week n Signals. Signalling certificate received from Petawawa. More parcels from friends at home. Saturday night picket duty again in Folkestone.

December 18 to 23, 1916   Interesting though very elementary course in Musketry. Bad weather hindered the finishing-up part at the ranges. Have passed on now to No. 2 squad with 100% standing. Sent home a cable for Christmas.

December 24, 1916   Christmas Sunday has been spent very quietly, but with lots of good cheer supplied by greetings and parcels received from kind friends at home.

December 25, 1916   Christmas in England has been indeed a green Christmas. No snow or ice, no sparkling frost or merry sleigh bells. But nice weather, nevertheless, barring light rainfall in the morning. It was a disappointment that Doug and I could not spend the day together. But neither of us has been able to procure a pass. A big Christmas meal was served to the Battery in two huts specially decorated for the purpose; this I missed, however, since by "Shorty" Mason's kindness I spent the afternoon and evening at his sister's place in Hythe. This introduced a very pleasant touch of home life into my Christmas. Letter from Bun Aiken.

December 26 to 28, 1916   Back to Signals with No. 2 squad. On Wednesday the 27th I had supper with Capt. and Harry Firth, Bob Fratt, Alex Fleming, Bill Henderson and Alan Cameron and spent the evening with Gerald Preston. Have made application for a New Year's leave to visit Doug at Hastings.

December 29, 1916   Off to St. Leonard's on a six-day pass! Left Shorncliffe at 9 o'clock, changed trains at Ashford and arrived at Hastings about noon. Discovered Doug comfortably billeted at 25 De Cham Rd., St. Leonard's. Hastings and St. Leonard's are really one town under two names and they are a very attractive place to live in or visit. A beautiful sea front, fine business streets and residential districts, and many nearby places of historic interest (Battle Abbey, Hastings Castle, etc.).

December 30, 1916   Doug was free most of today and we spent a happy time together. A picture show, municipal orchestra, etc. A bad cold is making things a little uncomfortable for me.

December 31, 1916   Last day of the old year! Marched to church today with No. 8 platoon of C.C.D. and felt very proud to parade with so many veterans.

January 1, 1917   A fine, bright New Year's Day. Went on a tour through Hastings Castle and the St. Clement's Caves. Cold much worse, so arranged to sleep tonight at a private hotel (Mrs. Finch, Abbotsford, 31 Warrior Square).

January 3, 1917   Yesterday Doug was on guard duty, so I put in a lazy time writing letters and reading current English periodicals and newspapers. Slept again at #31. Today Doug was free from duty and we were together again. Saw the pantomime "Red Riding Hood" and went again to hear the orchestra. I'll spend the night with Doug at his billet.

January 4, 1917   Left Doug at 8:30 this morning to catch my train at Hastings Stn. Reached Shorncliffe at noon and had to proceed at once to Hythe to fire off the ranges. Too late for the shorter distances but fired at 300 and 400 yds with fair results. Some of my mail went on to St. Leonard's and will have to be sent back to me. Found my hut (B9) quarantined but was allowed to "escape" to another hut.

January 12, 1917   Have been on a Gunnery course all this week. Yesterday I found my name on a list of 75 men who will be leaving soon for France. Sorry to go with my course not entirely finished, but if my immediate services are needed "at the front" I cannot complain. It will be hard on the folks at home. Wired the news at once to Doug.

January 13, 1917   Delightfully surprised this morning to have Doug drop in. I did not think he would be able to get leave. Have bequeathed to him much of my surplus baggage. A box from Aunt Minnie and Lottie Finlay arrived this evening and was a real treat for us both.

January 14, 1917   Afternoon and evening with Doug. We had tea with Col. and Mrs. Preston. Doug had to leave on the 8:19 train.

January 18, 1917   Still at Shorncliffe but have word that we are to leave for France early tomorrow. Mailed home my diary (Vol.1) and wrote letters home and to Ross and Doug. Here's wishing myself and all of us a speedy return!

POSTED TO FRANCE

January 19-20, 1917   Leaving Shorncliffe about 5:30 a.m., we journeyed by train to Southampton where we arrived at 10:30. The voyage across the Channel was made by night and in the early morning we marched over the 7-mile distance to the Canadian Base Depot, arriving about 8 o'clock. We are quartered for the time being in tents.

January 21, 1917   Since yesterday we have been under orders to proceed up to the 1st D.A.C. (Divisional Ammunition Column) tonight and so have drawn full active service equipment including steel helmet, gas mask, field dressing, "Kitchener" boots and fifty rounds of ammunition. However, counter-orders have cancelled the journey indefinitely, so we are to have at least one more night here at the base. The mud is bad though there has been little rain since our arrival. But there are conveniences that we did not have even in Shorncliffe and everything seems to be well organized in spite of the very large number of troops in camp. The countryside is much like Old

Ontario and it is hard to believe that we are really in France on the last stage of our journey to the firing line. Am sleeping with Harold Wilkinson (formerly at Orangeville High School and a brother of Frank of the 67th [later killed in action]) and several 67th men are quartered nearby.

January 23, 1917 At six o'clock last evening we paraded with full kit and an hour later marched off towards Le Havre. This time we went by a different route, passing through the village of Rouelles and arriving at Le Havre railway station about 9 o'clock, a 5-mile tramp. Entraining soon afterwards, we pulled out about midnight and found ourselves early this morning in Rouen (where Joan of Arc was tried and put to death many years ago). The greater part of today has been spent in the rest camp, near the Seine River.

By the tremendous amount of shipping that passes up and down one realizes the great commercial importance of this busy river. Several beautiful church towers could be seen in the distance. It was disappointing not to be free to wander about a little. We entrained again at about 5 pm. The weather is clear, cold and bright; like the Canadian winter, indeed, except for the lack of more snow than we see here.

January 24, 1917 Early morning found us at Abbéville on the Somme River. The weather is still bright and quite cold. Sleep last night was very difficult because of lack of heat; in other respects we are travelling comfortably in a modern third-class carriage. Plenty of food; issue plus purchased. Lengthy stops at Conteville, St. Pol and Bruay.

January 25, 1917   Disentrained this morning at Barlin, the present location of the 1st D.A.C. A brigade of 2nd Div. Artillery passed on its way back from the line. Did not recognize anyone I know, though I think the 14th Bty was with them. The intermittent roar of the guns is quite distinct from here. One or two Fritzie planes ventured across the line during the morning, followed by a long trail of white clouds from our anti-aircraft gunfire. Some 34 of our number have been attached to No. 3 Section of the D.A.C. in lines recently vacated by the 2nd Div. Column. The rest of us are with the 1st Section. Wilkinson, Ewart, Welford, and Kulp are still with me.

January 26, 1917   The weather remains clear and very frosty with quite a sprinkling of snow on the ground; typical January weather back in Ontario. Our section is billeted comfortably in the bare upstairs rooms of French dwellings in the village. There is no indication of our proceeding to the batteries immediately. Am detailed for 24-hour guard duty, commencing 5:30 this evening. No mail yet; wrote home tonight.

January 28, 1917   On guard duty all day yesterday. Weather remains bright and very cold. This morning was spent handling ammunition; afternoon free. I attended a church service in the evening at the Y.M.C.A. Barlin seems to be inhabited by coal miners and their families. There are no shirkers in this country, even among its more humble people; all are united in the one great national cause, the expulsion of the Hun.

January 29, 1917   Letter received from Gerald Preston. Dr. Durkin, Veterinary Officer for this D.A.C., made his rounds in No.3 section today. No change in weather.

February 1, 1917   Transferred with some twenty others to No. 2 section. Welford is still with me, but the change has separated us from Wilkinson and Kulp. Quartered in shacks, not very far distant from No. 3. Work much the same; handling ammunition to feed the guns up the line.

February 3, 1917   Weather, work, state of health, etc. no change. Also no mail from home, to my considerable disappointment. I learn that Gerald P. is now right section commander in the 6th Bty. Here's hoping it may be my good fortune to be sent to that unit.

February 5, 1917   This morning friend Welford left for "up the line." I hope that I may follow him before long. Received a letter from Doug; nothing from home yet. I find that Jack McLaren (from the 67th and formerly from Orangeville) is here in No.2 Section.

February 8, 1917   A letter from Ross and another one from Doug received today, the latter containing two recent letters from Mother. This is my first news from home for almost a month and is indeed a welcome treat.

February 11, 1917   Following an exceptionally heavy frost Friday night the weather has moderated quickly; today has been just like a mild, sunny spring day at home. Have been given a team of horses, temporarily, I hope. Had a short note from John Macpherson.

"UP THE LINE WITH THE BEST OF LUCK"

February 13, 1917   "Up the line with the best of luck" to the 9th Bty C.F.A., presently quite near me here in Hersin. A welcome change, especially since I find that this is an original Toronto battery and is still composed largely of Toronto men. Harold Wilkinson's brother, Russ, is a signaller in this unit and I find many of my Shorncliffe friends quartered in the same town. Burns and Black and Unwin are with me.

February 14, 1917   St. Valentine's Day has brought me good luck; John Macpherson is stationed quite near me here and we got together for a very pleasant reunion this evening. John is going to try for a transfer to the 9th. Am sleeping in a capacious loft above an old French dwelling; quite comfortable, for the duration of the good weather at least. Fine, bright spring weather continues, with cold nights. Excellent horse lines for the Bty.

February 15, 1917   Black and I have been taken on definitely to the B.C. (Battery Commander's) Party; we shall probably be here at the wagon lines for a week or so yet before taking our turn at the guns. Was privileged to see Sir Douglas

Haig at close range today, as he passed through on a tour of inspection. Surely his jolly smile was indeed "the smile of victory." His appearance inspires one with confidence in his leadership.

February 16, 1917   This afternoon a half-holiday was proclaimed and I rode down to Barlin to cash two English postal orders from Doug. Tonight I am for horse picket duty, probably my last, since Signallers are usually exempted from this job.

February 19, 1917   Have entered upon quite a new and unexpected experience, to last probably a week or two. Leaving the wagon lines at noon today, a party of eleven of us, with Lt. Higgins in charge, journeyed to some new gun positions west of Souchez. Our work is to dig fortified emplacements for a 4.5˙ Howitzer battery (perhaps ours) to take over in the near future. Already the valley in which we are to work, and adjacent valleys, are occupied by a number of batteries of various calibres which this evening opened up quite a heavy bombardment on enemy positions beyond Vimy Ridge. It was my first experience of heavy artillery fire at close range and proved a bit disconcerting for a moment. One soon becomes accustomed to the noise, however, and it did not seriously disturb my sleep during the night in a rough dug-out under the slope of the hill. Burns and Black are with me.

February 20, 1917   Our arduous task is evidently to be carried on in the midst of a veritable sea of the stickiest kind of mud caused by the recent thaw and present rainy weather. The whole countryside is a desolate ruin, showing unmistakable evidence of very severe fighting earlier in the war. The fields and hillsides are pocked with shell-holes and lined with the networks of old trenches. Where once stood happy villages now only battered walls and ruined streets remain. Here and there by the wayside a rude cross marks the lonely grave of some departed hero. The civilian population has long since gone to places more remote from the front line. Now at last we are experiencing real active service conditions, although as yet Fritz has not attempted any retaliation for the fire of our guns here.

February 21, 1917   This afternoon I spent some time at the ruined village of Ablain-St. Nazaire, to which place our building materials are brought up on a little narrow-gauge railway line. Quite near the railhead is a pathetic little graveyard, one of so many in this stricken country. All about the scattered mounds with their rough crosses lie gaping shell-holes and rusted barbed wire and ruined entrenchments, while the inscriptions on the crosses bear simple but impressive witness to the glorious end of the soldiers of France sleeping below.

February 23, 1917   A small Y.M.C.A. canteen, situated in the ruined remnant of a demolished house down in the village, supplies us with a few simple luxuries to supplement our rather unsatisfying rations. But alas! Lack of transportation facilities will soon necessitate the closing up of this convenient source and we shall have to depend on the generosity of our friends back at the wagon lines. However, our lot is not so very pitiable as to justify complaint. We are doing a necessary job, in which we have now the help of five more men recently arrived; and weather conditions have not continued to be hopelessly unfavourable. The sun has kept consistently behind the clouds and mist, but there has not been much rain since the first day or two and the valley is beginning to dry up. Indeed, I am quite enjoying the experience here, even though we have to live like cliff-dwellers.

February 24, 1917   It is certainly a wonder that Fritz does not send over "a few." We are only a scant 1800 yards from the front-line trenches and, daily, heavy artillery fire is directed at the enemy from the various batteries all around us. However, far be it from us to complain about this lack of recognition on the part of our German opponents. Doubtless the time will come when they will not be slow to reply to our advances.

February 25, 1917   Whether the importance of the work we are doing justifies it or not, we had to carry on today (Sunday) just as usual. This was a distinct disappointment, for I had confidently counted on having a spare hour in which to journey down to a "wee bit creek" and indulge in a general clean-up. My appearance, with a week's growth of beard on my face and my uniform plentifully besprinkled with mud, cannot be very presentable. I have contrived to save the situation somewhat by overalls beautifully modeled out of a few sand bags; the result reminds one of a Texan bronco-buster. This afternoon the sun came out at last and shone down approvingly on the work we have done. The return of fair weather brought out quite a swarm of aeroplanes, but I don't think that Fritz has been able yet to come close enough to observe our new positions here.

A walk up the war-scarred hillside above our humble dwelling reveals a pitiful yet glorious tale of terrible hand-to-hand encounters between French and German forces back in the 1915 campaign. The details of the scene are unpleasant; yet in the midst of all the desolation I found one pretty little yellow spring flower peeping towards the sky. Surely a harbinger of better things to come.

March 2, 1917   Our work is progressing favourably and it looks as though we shall not be here much longer. Rumours continue to reach us to the effect that the Battery is likely to move soon from its present position at Aix-Noulette. Where we shall go into action next is a matter of conjecture; popular opinion is divided between Mont St. Eloi and Armentières. Weather conditions remain satisfactory, bright sunshine days predominating. Fritz occasionally sends over a few shells into our neighbourhood, with negligible results. The aeroplanes are very active along the front. I am delighted to find that H.E. Jarrett of the 9th formerly served for nine months under Ross in the Pats. Have had several interesting chats with him. No home mail yet.

March 4, 1917   The conclusion of a full day's work today found our six gun pits pretty well completed and tonight five of us have journeyed by G.S. wagon back to Hersin, arriving about nine o'clock. Angus's birthday is affectionately remembered. He has been a wonderful older brother to all the rest of us.

March 5, 1917   The old routine of harness-cleaning and attending the B.C. Party horses! A snowfall last night has raised up quite a layer of mud again; evidently March weather, as at home, will not be all pleasant. The Battery is to move somewhere soon. Was delighted to meet W.P. Buchanan, formerly of Carlton School, Toronto, over at the Y this evening. He is with the 75th Bn and went through some heavy fighting recently. [Buchanan was killed in action a month later.]

March 7, 1917   This morning I was detailed to proceed with an advance party to a new battery position. Set out about 9:30 a.m. on bicycles with Mason, McClelland, and Sgt. Adams. A stop for minor repairs early in the journey caused me to lose the rest of the party and I followed alone. The name of our destination was unknown to me, but a general idea that we were to go into the St. Eloi area led me up through Servins and Villers-au-Bois and over to Chamblain d'Abbé, where I caught up with my companions about 1 p.m. We continued south about a mile in the general direction of Arras and spent the afternoon putting up tents for the Battery wagon lines along the edge of a wood.

March 8, 1917   A frosty night was followed this morning by a snowfall and warmer weather. The left section of the

Battery arrived from Hersin about noon. I don't feel any ill effects of yesterday's uphill trip of some 12 or 15 kilometers, though it was my first ride on a bicycle for a year or more and I had most of my kit with me.

March 9, 1917   This morning the rest of the Battery arrived and with it came my first two letters from home, dated February 7 and 11; very gladly received. Surely earlier mail will soon come along from Shorncliffe. The Battery, with Black and myself in the B.C. Party, went up the line late this afternoon and took up a position in an old infantry reserve trench southeast of Mont St. Eloi and some 3000 yds. from enemy lines. Slept in an old dug-out, rather damp but fairly comfortable.

March 10, 1917   Most of the day has been spent improving gun-pits and (by the signallers) laying lines of communication. This afternoon I located Bun Aiken over at the 14th Bty position and had a very pleasant chat with him. He informs me that the 3rd Division is coming to this front very shortly, so I should soon see Ross and other chaps from home.

March 11, 1917   On 24-hour telephone duty at the gun positions with Black. We are not firing a great deal yet and the work is quite light but interesting. Our sleeping quarters (in the signal dug-out) are reasonably comfortable and the weather is fair and warm.

March 15, 1917   On battery duty again today and tonight. I am assured that the 3rd Division is to come in near here, so I hope soon to get in touch with Ross. Letter from Uncle Arthur but no more word from home yet.

March 17, 1917   My twenty-second birthday has been celebrated on O.P. (Observation Post) duty close behind the front-line trenches. It proved quite an interesting experience, though punctuated by one or two close calls from Fritz's whiz bangs. German aeroplanes of the latest type (The Red Devils, under Richthofen, as I found out later on) are playing havoc with our scout planes, which lack both the speed and the manoeuverability of their opponents.

March 13, 1917   Up the line again this afternoon, this time on liaison duty with the infantry for four days with Lt. Higgins and Black. Our dug-out is comfortable and reasonably safe, situated in a support trench in front of 13th Bn Headquarters. This area seems to be shelled daily, but no great chance of damaging our position to any extent. Our Divisional front extends, I think, from Neuville-St.Vaast south to Meurie, facing Thélus still in enemy hands. The trenches are decidedly muddy.

March 21, 1917   We witnessed a heavy "strafe" and an attempted attack on our left front early this morning. The Red Devils were very active. Cold nights and the necessity for continuous telephone and observation duties are our chief hardships here. Snow and rain yesterday.

March 22, 1917   Our four-day duty ended at 4 p.m. today, with a long muddy walk back to the Battery.

March 23, *1917*   A red-letter day today, for I have at last found brother Ross. Leaving the Battery in the early afternoon, I tramped across country beyond Mont St. Eloi and finally located the Pats just arrived from Bruay. Our meeting seemed almost too good to be true and is more like a dream than a reality even yet. Ross looks to be in splendid health despite his twenty months' campaigning; but I wish he could be freed from it all, now that I am here to represent the family. Met Alf Warman, who was assistant caretaker at Annette.

March 24, *1917*   Ross's birthday today, unfortunately, finds me on battery duty again, so I cannot get over to celebrate it with him. Fritz's heavies have been directed intermittently against Mont St. Eloi, but I very much hope they did not reach the Pats. Tonight at 11 o'clock our time went ahead one hour to comply with the French adoption, for a second year, of the Daylight Saving System. Fritz's planes made several daring observation tours during this afternoon, so we may reasonably expect more (and more accurate) enemy shell-fire shortly.

March 26, *1917*   All available men have been busy handling ammunition throughout yesterday and today. A constant flow of this very necessary item has been pouring in nightly, until now we have 1500 to 2000 rounds per gun ready to send over to Fritz. I think the beginning of the big push is near at hand.

March 27, 1917   On battery duty again with Black. Early this morning twelve new men reported for duty on the two new guns that are to arrive today, for now we are to be a six-gun battery. Among the newcomers were Duke, Strachan, Brown, Wilson and Yule of the 67th. Unfortunately, it was later discovered that this was not the group that should have reported here, a mistake having been made down at the base. So the abovementioned friends had to go back to the D.A.C. tonight. It is a disappointment that Duke at least could not have stayed with the Battery; I hope he may be sent up again later.

March 28, 1917   Walked to St. Eloi again this afternoon but found to my disappointment Companies 1 and 4 of the Pats had gone up the line last night for five days. On my return journey I ran across F. Ferguson (of Orangeville B.C.), with whom I had quite a pleasant chat. Tried to find Bun Aiken again but his battery had moved. Late at night the mail delivery brought me many letters long looked for: 19 in number. It certainly provided me with a wonderful treat. Shall be very busy answering all these epistles.

March 29, 1917   Very wet and muddy "on our street" this morning, but I have at last managed to draw a pair of larrigans and can defy the inclement weather. Tonight I went up with a working party and helped carry ammunition to prospective gun positions a few hundred yards back of the line. We were greeted by a very lively barrage of shells directed at our support trenches by friend Fritz and had to await his pleasure before carrying on with our work. Rain and mud certainly add <u>zest</u> to our various labours recently.

March 31, 1917   Four new signallers reported from the D.A.C. for duty with our battery, one being Allan Cameron, newly arrived from Shorncliffe. Am still in luck in linking up with old friends. About 7 o'clock tonight guns of the right of our position (probably near Arras) opened up a terrific fire on enemy lines: a foretaste of what is soon to come, I imagine. All indications point to an early opening of the great offensive.

April 1, 1917   Battery duty again with Black. How I long for a real Sunday! Here things go on just as on weekdays and the Sabbath slips by almost unnoticed. Today is Palm Sunday and next Friday is Easter Day. I am wondering if this sacred season will be celebrated here by comparative peace and quietness or by the very climax of this terrible war of the nations. Last night's mail brought me five more letters; in my spare time in the silent (?) hours of the night I must try to answer a few of them.

April 2, 1917   I wandered many weary miles today in a vain effort to locate the P.P.s, who I found have moved to parts unknown. Following all available clues, I trudged through this most atrocious French mud to St. Eloi, to Ecoivres, to Bruay, to Maroeuil, and back to the Battery. It was a disappointment not to find Ross, for I had been counting on seeing him today ever since my last trip to St. Eloi. Two Fritzie observation balloons destroyed.

April 4, 1917   Following a lively scrap with a small fast Fritz machine, one of our battle planes was forced to come down just fifty yards in advance of our guns. The pilot, fatally wounded, made a wonderfully good landing on difficult ground. It was a real sorrow to learn of his death at a field dressing station some hours later. The observer, an R.F.C. sergeant, escaped unhurt. One of the craft's machine guns had jammed at a critical moment in the fight.

I have volunteered to go forward with Lt. Evans, liaison officer, when the big push begins; it will be dangerous work, but I feel it a duty to take my share of the risks. Curiously, I'm not worried about possible consequences to myself, though I realize the cost at which victory will be gained against a strongly prepared enemy.

Tonight's mail brought me three parcels; much delicious "eats" and many useful articles contained therein.

April 5, 1917   Five Fritzies surrendered on this front, following an exceptionally heavy bombardment by our guns this morning. They are said to have reported dissatisfaction among enemy troops. Is this a local grievance, or does it indicate a state of demoralization that might make resistance to our advance less strenuous than expected?

April 6, 1917   Good Friday in the trenches! Black and I are on battery duty. It is well that this is indoor duty for there are letters which I ought to write before the "big push" begins. It seems likely now that the Easter season will be over before things start to move. Our artillery continues to be quite active and Fritz makes no mean retaliation.

April 7, 1917 News reaches us of Uncle Sam's declaration of war on Germany on April 4th. This should shorten the war, though I guess <u>we'll</u> finish the job on this western front before his newly created armies can join us. Am making all haste to write as many letters as possible now, for doubtless opportunities for writing will soon be few and far between.

April 8, 1917 Today is Easter Sunday, but I have hardly had time to stop and think of its significance. At 11 a.m. the party warned for liaison duty left the battery in order to be in position for the advance on the morrow. Our route took us up Sapper Ave. and Douai Trench into the extensive tunnel system that has been built to join the support trenches to the front line. These long, deep, electric-lighted underground passageways are quite a triumph of the art of engineering and should be of great value in launching the attack. Our wires are all connected and ready to take over the top after the infantry gets moving.

THE BATTLE OF VIMY RIDGE

April 9, 1917 This has been a great day. Last night was spent half-reclining in a narrow offshoot of the tunnel with the 13th Bn men who were to go over in the first wave of the attack. Sleep was, of course, out of the question. As dawn approached, the infantrymen lined up quietly along the main corridor and filed silently up the steps into the front-line trench. At precisely 5:30 a.m. our artillery fire, which up till then had been only spasmodic, broke out in a terrific roar. Almost immediately the infantry went over the top, following closely on the curtain of artillery fire which gradually lifted farther and farther forward. The first wave of the attack carried the first and second German lines, where the most determined opposition was met, and then pushed on towards the enemy supporting troops, while the second wave, advancing overland from our support lines, followed on in the rear, ready to go through to the second objective. At about 7 o'clock, just as the third wave was preparing to advance, Mr. Evans and his trusty henchmen clambered over the parapet with heavy reels of wire and pushed forward into enemy country. Nothing could equal the scene of destruction and desolation wrought by the terrific concentration of our gunfire and by the fury of the infantry attack. German artillery fire was still intense but poorly directed; after the first resistance the Germans appeared to be giving way on all sides and our casualties were remarkably light. Prisoners picked their way in groups towards our rear or aided in the removal of our wounded from the battlefield. Our party soon had telephone communication established up to the Black Line, and Fallis and I went on with Lt. Evans to a point well forward, from which we could follow events and signal back by flag.

We were all continuously under quite a heavy counter-barrage, but during the entire day none of our party was hurt. By early afternoon practically all our objectives were attained all along the line. On the left we could see the troops swarming up and over the highest points on Vimy Ridge; on the right the attack was likewise pushed home. Prisoners, guns and ammunition fell into our hands in large numbers and quantity. At night our party established a L.O. HQ in the Red Line and we had the satisfaction of sleeping in a deep, comfortable Fritzie dug-out, perfectly content with the day's work and humbly thankful for being still alive and unhurt when so many had paid the price. Snow and rain at night; lost for half an hour and lucky to get back to the dug-out.

April 10, 1917   This afternoon we went back to the Battery, established in its new position immediately in rear of our former front line. Wet, muddy weather has spoiled our chances of pushing on to further victories just now. The roads and fields are impassable, even for field artillery. Slept comfortably in signal dug-out.

April 11, 1917   A day of rest for the liaison party. Discovered a good dug-out in Fritzie's old line and several of us made it our temporary home.

April 13, 1917   On battery duty with Drew. Muddy weather continues, to everybody's disappointment.

April 14, 1917   Just at midnight last night came orders for the Battery to move to a new position, two miles farther, immediately. Drew and I have been left at the old position to maintain communications with the wagon lines.

April 16, 1917   This evening the Battery moved forward again, this time to a position just behind the railway embankment at Farbus. Drew and I are still back here running our own little show, but doubtless we shall go forward tomorrow.

April 17, 1917   Up to the Battery this afternoon, taking up $1\frac{1}{2}$ miles of wire on our way. I suffered the loss of my extra haversack en route and with it my writing case, maps and various souvenirs. I find that Allan Cameron was slightly wounded last night and went back to a dressing station in the rear. Most of the B.C. Party are living in dug-outs under a very strong Fritzie whiz-bang position captured on the 9th with all guns intact (up on the crest in Farbus Wood).

April 18, 1917   Evidently we are in a rather exposed position and our guns have to maintain a discreet silence for the time being. Fritz's shells are constantly dropping uncomfortably near; one of the 12th Bty guns moving into position behind us, was wrecked by a direct hit and six men were wounded. Three 9th Bty men received "Blighty's" today. A beautiful stretch of open country lies ahead, with numerous towns and villages. Chiefly a mining country, judging by the slag heaps dotting the landscape. A corner of Lens is visible away to the north; ahead lie Willerval, Arleux, Fresnoy, Oppy, Neuvireuil, etc. Doubtless our objective on this front is the important town of Douai. There is sure to be a desperate resistance offered to our further advance.

April 20, 1917   On battery duty with Drew. Guns registered this morning: 43 rounds in 15 minutes. Wrote my first letter home since the 8th of the month. Allan Cameron returned to duty.

April 23, 1917   Heavy fighting on our right flank. We learn that the Germans are counter-attacking in force. The usual number of "wampers", shrapnel, etc. have fallen in our vicinity.

April 24, 1917   From a point of vantage on the Ridge this afternoon I watched a battalion of German infantry make a counter-attack to the south of Oppy. They must have suffered heavily under our artillery fire and evidently failed to retake any lost ground.

April 25, 1917   One more of our battle planes was brought down by a speedy Fritz today. Our air losses must have been terrific during the past two months. Always it is the slow, low-flying "buzz wagons" that are being sacrificed to obtain badly needed information. All honour to them!

April 26, 1917   Saw two more of our planes come down in flames and another one forced to land in enemy lines. What heroes these flying men are! Our faster planes are operating far into Fritz's country.

April 27, 1917   On battery duty again, this time with Dunbar. Fritz seems particularly anxious to keep our observation planes back today; probably he is making some extensive changes in the disposition of troops and guns, for defense or offense, I wonder? Rather heavy strafing today, with more casualties in the battery behind us (the 12th). <u>Our</u> next "show" commences tomorrow morning, unless again postponed.

April 28, 1917   Preceded by the usual overwhelming artillery preparation, commencing 4:25 a.m., the infantry on our immediate front advanced and captured Arleux, thus straightening out the line to conform to recent gains on our right flank. The 16th and 10th Battalions were two of the units that went "over the top." As expected, our losses from the machine gun fire in the captured village were heavy. Fritz's counter-barrage was weak, however, and only a few scattered shells came back even to our advanced artillery positions; but counter attacks must be expected. Dunbar and I carried on with telephone duties at the Battery last night and early morning. At midnight I went up the hill to Bde HQ with a message through a considerable barrage; was able to get around the worst spots. Letter from Ewart received this morning, dated at Sandling Camp April 23rd but written on board the *Carpathia*. Tonight from about 8:30 to 9:00 Fritz shelled our new line very heavily, but no infantry came over to retake the ground we won this morning. McKen wounded.

April 29, 1917   A beautiful, warm day with a fresh breeze blowing and the artillery on both sides comparatively quiet. Worked on a digging party all afternoon and evening, endeavouring to make the cook house (such as it is) more safe from hostile shells. It would be the height of disaster if our rations were blown up! Met Lt. Bill Munroe, formerly of the 67th but now with the 15th Bn. [Bill Munroe was killed the following day.]

May 2, 1917   On O.P. duty with Adams on the ridge to the right rear of the Battery. Lt. Hampshire is F.O.O. From about 11:30 a.m. to 2 p.m. an enemy heavy battery located at Izel on our distant right front carried on a very thorough bombardment of our battery position and succeeded in putting one of our guns out of action and knocking in several dugouts. No casualties occurred, as our men quickly retired to safety until Fritz's wrath was appeased. Our naval guns finally reached the offending battery and we were able to assemble for a belated dinner and to make repairs to gunpits and dugouts. The trail of the demolished gun was found on the other side of the railway embankment fifty yards away. Preparations are under way for another attack tomorrow on this front.

May 3, 1917   The attack this morning opened up at 3:45, infantry and artillery again combining in another sturdy push. Before noon our front was extending beyond Fresnoy and the troops on our left made a corresponding gain. On the right British troops failed for a second time to capture Oppy, which is very strongly held with wire entanglements and machine guns. This leaves us temporarily in a salient. The German defense all along the line was more stubborn than before, but our push went forward all the same and we netted a considerable number of prisoners. I had very little to do during the day, but at 6 o'clock this evening I went on liaison duty with Dunbar and two signallers from each of the other 3rd Bde batteries under Lt. Richardson of the 10th. Tonight I am in an ex-German dug-out just on the edge of Arleux, alternating on the telephone and observation duty and sleeping. Had two very close "shaves" from the whiz-bangs, the nearest one bursting only three or four yards away. A steel helmet is quite a protection at such times. Hope Ross came through okay.

May 4, 1917   Quite a number of 5.9s came uncomfortably close this a.m., one burying a man and giving him a bad "shell shock." No exciting developments during the day. Dunbar and I went out to inspect the wire in the afternoon and repaired all breaks in the triple-line ladder system that has been established back to the first intermediate station. The value of this system was made evident by a number of breaks that had occurred without interrupting communications. About 7:30 p.m. we were relieved and journeyed back to our own battery quarters, dodging some shrapnel on the way.

May 5, 1917   Hot, summerlike weather made possible an open air bath in shell-hole water this morning. In the evening a freshening breeze brought a brief little sun shower. For me it has been a day of rest, much appreciated after the strenuous duties of a 24-hour liaison. Conditions are much quieter along our front, though our position has been sprinkled with shrapnel at intervals. Present indications suggest a move for the Battery in the very near future to parts unknown. Some thunder and lightning this afternoon.

May 6, 1917   German 4.1 and 5.9 batteries played havoc with our gun positions for two hours this afternoon. One more gun put out of action. No casualties.

May 7, 1917   On battery duty with Bill Adams from 9 o'clock to 1 p.m. Our position and the two remaining guns have been taken over by D65 R.F.A. and we have moved north a mile or so to Vimy Station, taking over three guns formerly manned by D15 R.F.A Thus our battery is now supporting 2nd Div. infantry, the 1st Division having withdrawn from the Fresnoy line. A few hundred yards to the rear is the highest part of Vimy Ridge.

This evening some of the signallers were sent back to the wagon lines for a rest. So here we are, back near the Nine Elms (or where the Nine Elms used to be), still within sound and reach of the screeching shells but unlikely to be molested by them at this distance. Furthermore, we are in tents once again. An agreeable change after the dug-outs and gun-pits that have been our home for so long. Mail from home, both this morning and this evening.

May 8, 1917   Rain, all last night and this morning! Yesterday the Battery suffered a loss in the death of Bdr. Jim Allen, who was killed by a shell near the old Battery position at Farbus. This afternoon he was buried, in the presence of all at the

W.L. (wagon lines), among other fallen heroes on the open battlefield close to the Arras-Lens road. Allen was an original 9th Battery man, a good soldier and well liked by everybody. Fresnoy was retaken by the enemy today.

May 9, 1917 Another <u>big</u> day, for most of it has been spent with Captain Ross Macpherson, whom I located with his company just north of Neuville-St. Vaast. He is looking very fit. Beaucoup gas and H.E. shells were thrown at us during the day and evening. No damage done.

May 11, 1917 An interesting morning on the range-finder. Most of our time here, however, has been devoted to the care of our "long-faced friends," the two B.C. Party chargers. More letters from home.

May 12, 1917 Spent a couple of hours with Ross again this evening. It was fortunate that I was able to go over to see him at this time, for I found No.4 Co. under orders to go up to the front line tonight.

May 14, 1917 The wagon lines were moved over near Neuville-St. Vaast to escape possible damage from the occasional long-range shells that Fritz is still sending over. We are quite pleasantly situated now, overlooking green fields instead of a desolate waste of shell-holes. Of course, the old trenches and ruined houses are still with us, but time and the transforming touch of spring have already worked wonders. Heavy rain today, with cooler weather. Two parcels gratefully received.

May 16, 1917   Spent yesterday with Cpl. Bristow re-establishing communications between our W.L. and Bde HQ. This afternoon Sgt. Henderson and Black came back to the W.L. and Bristow and I went up to the guns. Commenced a 24-hour Bde O.P. duty at 6:30. More rain.

May 18, 1917   On battery O.P. duty this afternoon with Major Cook. Dunbar and Baillie have been awarded the M.M. [military medal].

May 20, 1917   On battery duty with Baillie today. He and Dunbar were officially decorated this evening.

May 23, 1917   Saw Gerald Preston and Stuart Porter today. They informed me that Dr. Carson is M.O. of the 1st Bde C.F.A.

May 24, 1917   On liaison duty with McClennan since early this morning. Bright sunshine and a cool breeze; just like a typical Victoria Day at home.

May 25, 1917   Had the pleasure today of reading part of a very fine book, *A Student in Arms*, by Donald Hankey.

June 2, 1917   This morning we were subjected to a prolonged and violent bombardment by Heinie's 4.1s and 5.9s. Even our deep dug-outs under the railway embankment were in imminent danger of destruction. One shell did make a break in the ceiling of the gunner's section. It seemed little short of a miracle that we suffered no loss, either of men or guns. Some casualties are reported in the 1st Div. Bn, newly arrived to relieve the 2nd Div.

June 3, 1917   Fritz still continues to lavish his attention on us here at all hours of the day and night. This afternoon Dr. Carson called to see me and told me Bun Aiken had been wounded. Am on battery duty with Smith today. Our right section moved north some two or three miles after dark this evening; we follow tomorrow.

June 4, 1917   Bristow, Dunbar and Baillie went on to the new positions early this afternoon, leaving Bdr. Pallett, Smith and myself to follow with the left section and the balance of our signalling equipment tonight. The wagons and limbers came up about 10 p.m. and were just about to move off when a hostile plane evidently spotted us from above (aided by the light of a full moon) and dropped on us its whole cargo of heavy bombs, six in all. A terrible scene followed. The concussion was terrific and I was saved only by being on the opposite side of a G.S. wagon from that on which the bombs fell some ten or twelve yards away. When the heavy pall of black smoke lifted, the few of us who were left unhurt joined in attending to the wounded. We found three dead: Cpl. Lemon, Bdr. Conroy, and Gnr. McIsaac. 24 others were more or less badly wounded, including Pallett (an easy "Blighty" I think), Myers, Norman, Sager, Errington and Brooks. The nearest dressing station was in Vimy village; and there I escorted Pallett and Brooks and later helped carry poor Errington, pretty well done for, I fear. By good fortune neither Hampshire nor MacPherson (two of our officers) was badly hurt and they with Sgt. Petrie and Cpl. McChesney took charge of the situation. The horse casualties were heavy, but a sufficient number were still available to pull away with one gun and one G.S. wagon. Smith and I reopened communications with Bde and stayed the night. Luckily, Allan Cameron was with the right section at the new gun position. I thank God most humbly that I was so wonderfully spared the fate of so many of my comrades in the disaster.

June 5, 1917   My head throbs with the heavy concussion of last night, but otherwise I am O.K. After dark this evening the remaining gun was taken to the new position and one G.S. load followed. Some of our equipment is still left over and once again I am detailed to stay behind, this time with Dunbar, who walked back here with Cpl. Bristow.

June 6, 1917   At noon today Lister arrived from the W.L. with a party of new gunners and several of my fellow signallers. Among the gunners I was delighted to find Jack McLaren, whom I had last seen at No. 1 section of the D.A.C. Dunbar went along with the newcomers to guide them to our new Battery position, leaving Burns to stay here with me. At night a G.S. wagon arrived, already well loaded and unable to carry to the guns much additional equipment. So here we are, still stranded in this place of horrible memory. Have learned to my sorrow that Errington and Pidgely have both died of their wounds.

June 7, 1917   Saw Stuart Porter again today and found him still O.K. The expected G.S. wagon arrived about 10:30 and Burns and I followed it up to the new position. Got to bed about 1 o'clock.

June 8, 1917   This is a beautiful location. We are in a little valley, shaped like an amphitheatre, with the high crest of Vimy Ridge immediately behind us (making a very convenient O.P.) and the guns to the right firing over a little knoll which affords excellent concealment. The narrow outlet of our small world (for we are the sole inhabitants) opens out to the northeast into a great plain, with Lens well to the front but concealed from view by another little mound. Givenchy is on our left and Vimy village now to the right, with several other towns within easy range of our guns. Our guns are covering a 3rd Div. area at present held by Ross's brigade. Whether the P.P.'s are in the line or not I do not know. The signallers spent the day excavating a damaged portion of our dug-out. Most of us are living, in the meantime, in another old Fritzie dug-out in the hill at the rear. Both sides were busy cutting wire (with artillery fire) all day; just at dark this evening Fritz put up a heavy and prolonged barrage without much advantage to himself or disadvantage to us. Our return fire started a big blaze, probably an ammunition dump, in or near Lens.

June 9, 1917   It is reported that late last night our infantry carried out successful raids, penetrating to the enemy's third line. Yesterday's mail brought me letters from home, long delayed, confirming a report that Ewart had sent me of R.B. McGuire's accidental death in England, and I have discovered his name in the *Times* casualty list of May 18th. It is sad news indeed, and it makes one heavy at heart to realize what a terrible blow it must be to his people at home, who have already lost their oldest boy in this war. A sixth fatality has occurred from the tragedy of last Monday in the death of Cpl. Sykes. This afternoon Dunbar, Mason, Smith, and I moved down to the W.L. for a few days' rest. There is little work for the B.C. Party at the guns. On the way I learned that Ross had been on leave and had not yet returned; a Lance-corporal of No. 4 Co. of the Pats was my informant.

June 10, 1917   I set out to find John M. this afternoon, but learned that he is at Carency and decided to postpone the visit. With some difficulty I located the transport lines of the 7th Inf. Bde and left a note for Ross. I hope he returns soon, for word has arrived that we are pulling out of our present gun positions enroute for parts unknown.

June 11, 1917   An early shift on Bde W.L. telephone duty. This evening Mel Fydell called on me and I walked back with him to the D.A.C. lines, where we gathered together a number of the 67th Bty men (MacDonald, Stirrett, Duke and Begg) and exchanged news of many others. A very delightful evening. Two Fritz planes were brought down on our front today.

June 12, 1917   All our guns are back at the W.L. now and today we had an inspection by the Brigade Commander. Went over to the P.P. lines later but found Ross still away. I fear I may miss him if he does not return soon.

June 13, 1917   Major Cook summarily deposed Cpl. Bristow from his position as "O.C. SIGNALS" in absence of Sgt. Henderson; reason unknown as yet. To my amazement I was offered a stripe (as Bombardier) but did not feel justified in accepting it over the heads of more experienced men. Bill Adams was later placed temporarily in charge of the Party. Some army, when a man like Bristow is subjected to such unfair treatment! [Bristow later admitted being insubordinate to his superior.]

June 16, 1917   On Thursday (the 14th) we were inspected by Gen. Thacker. Were criticized for lack of small arms ammunition (for rifles). This afternoon and evening a Brigade Field Day was held with interesting contests (a "V.C." race, centipede race, etc.) and entertainment by the 4th Bn band and a concert party.

June 17, 1917   On Bde telephone duty from 1 to 7 a.m. Found Ross this morning and this afternoon we had quite a walk together in a vain effort to locate Gerald Preston and Dr. Carson; both 1st and 2nd Brigades had moved to new locations, so we were out of luck. A Canadian mail this evening brought a fitting conclusion to a perfect day.

June 19, 1917   Was with Ross again this evening and dined with the 4th Co. officers of the Pats. Visual signalling practice and fatigues are "the order of the day" for us during this rest. It is likely that we shall go back into action again soon.

June 21, 1917   Reported to the dental officer for treatment this a.m. but he was unable to take me on; so I spent the rest of the morning wandering through the 3rd Div. area, where I finally located the 33rd Bty. Had a long chat with H. Keith, L. Patterson, B. Booth and F. Jackson, all Orangeville boys. Missed Earl Stevenson, who was up at the guns. Mother's and Doug's birthdays today did not pass unnoticed.

June 22, 1917   The considerable rainfall of the last few days has brought cooler weather after a prolonged spell of heat. Had a tooth refilled by the dentist this morning. Our Brigade is now a part of the newly organized 4th Division artillery. Lots of parcels lately from various friends.

June 24, 1917   Brigade telephone duty, 1 to 7 a.m. Spent another couple of hours with Ross this afternoon; met Capt. Papineau (grandson of Louis Joseph Papineau, the French-Canadian "rebel" of 1837-8, and a very gallant officer). [Papineau was killed later at Passchendaele.] Witnessed an inspection of a special guard-of-honour (100 P.P. officers and men) chosen to go out to Houdain for the Duke of Connaught's visit by Col. Adamson and Major Gault. Princess Patricia's flag, with two or three shrapnel rents from the early days of the war, was borne proudly at the head of the detachment.

This evening, with Sgt. Henderson and seven other signallers, I went up to our former battery position where the

9th will go into action again for a few days before proceeding to the 4th Div. front. We took down our red patches (1st Div. insignia) on the morning parade; our new patches will be green. Spent the night under the stars, my best sleep for weeks.

June 25, 1917 Telephone wire strung up to a rear O.P. and all guns registered. Helped build a bivouac among the trees at the bottom of the slope, where McClennan and I spent the night protected from the heavy rain that fell at intervals.

June 26, 1917 Battery duty with McClennan. We enjoyed some delicious wild strawberries growing just back of the guns; it doesn't seem possible that there is a war on when one gets into such a delightful, secluded little valley as this. But at times the cold realities force themselves upon one even here and there is not much time for idling. Have read Harold Bell Wright's book, *When a Man's a Man*.

June 28, 1917 At midnight last night I was called out to go over to Bde HQ with Johnson, the orderly sergeant. On my return I watched the commencement of our barrage (2:30 a.m.) under cover of which the 3rd and the 4th Div. infantry captured Avion with, it is reported, few casualties and a considerable number of German prisoners. Went on battery duty with Bristow at 9 a.m.

June 29, 1917 With Sgt. Henderson and Colquhoun, I accompanied Major Cook and Lt. Macpherson on a reconnaissance for a new battery position. Made a second trip in the evening to the place chosen, but later the move was cancelled as taking us too far from the rest of the Bde. The position that was condemned was near Cité de Petit Bois, southeast of Liévin. Arrived back at the valley quite late.

June 30, 1917   Weather colder today, with much rain. At night we moved into new position at La Chaudière, Fosse 1, near the intersection of the Arras-Lens and Vimy roads. Rather unpleasant work in the dark and rain.

July 1, 1917   Dominion Day! After only an hour's sleep we were aroused at daybreak to dig in the guns and (for the B.C. Party) to construct a fire-control trench in the centre rear of the gun positions. The work occupied all morning. I took over battery duty with Cpl. Bristow. At noon precisely all the guns of the Canadian Corps opened fire in two resounding salvoes to commemorate another anniversary of Canada's birth spent by so many of her sons on the field of battle. It was a soul-stirring moment, which touched to the depths the emotions of us all, and must have given Fritz a terrific scare!

July 2, 1917   Came off battery duty at 9 a.m. and spent most of the day sleeping and cleaning up. In the evening I was instructed to go back to the W.L. for a rest and walked down with Lt. Higgins. Black, Baillie, and the two Wilkinsons went up for duty. The heavy work of the past week, along with a touch of "dug-out-itis" make this change very welcome.

July 5, 1917   On Bde telephone duty 1 to 7 a.m. Burns came through from the guns to report to Corps for a wireless course. Bdr. Bill Barker, another First Contingent man, was killed last night and one man wounded.

July 6, 1917   Rode to Mont St. Eloi with Bdr. Fallas today and passed the first civilians I have seen in three months. Had a close look at the ruins of the old church on the hill, a reminder of the ravages of the 1870 war.

July 8-12, 1917   This week commenced with an Anglican communion service on Sunday, my first in France. On Tuesday Allan Cameron was hit in the hand: the second time wounded since he came to France. Alex Fleming, Stuart Porter and Gerald Preston dropped in to see me. Lt. Hampshere of the 10th Bty was killed by a shell on Thursday.

July 13, 1917   Another turn on early Bde duty gave me the rest of the day free and I rode "Reuben" through Villers-au-Bois to the Chateau-de-la-Haie, where I found Ross very comfortably located for a few days' rest. The chateau and grounds are very beautiful and troops quartered in such surroundings are indeed fortunate. Ross is looking well as usual. I had lunch with No.4 officers and in the afternoon witnessed Gen. Macdonell's farewell inspection of the 7th Inf Bde, which he is now leaving for a higher command. On the way back in the evening I saw Bert Booth and Lloyd Patterson again, also Rogers and Perc McLean. A very delightful day's outing!

July 15, 1917   Church Parade this p.m. Heavy rain at intervals. Lt. Evans was wounded yesterday.

July 21, 1917   Still at the W.L. Weather very changeable all week, but mostly wet and blustery. Allan Cameron was sent to the rest camp on Wednesday (18th) for treatment of his wounded hand. "Shorty" Mason called to see me this evening and gave me news of many other 67th fellows.

July 22, 1917   Ross rode over to see me in the early morning and I went with him (on my long-faced friend Reuben) to 1st Bde HQ where we found Dr. Carson. Walked over to 33rd Bty W.L. and saw Lloyd Patterson again.

July 24, 1917   I returned to the guns yesterday afternoon. One year ago today I reported for duty with the 67th Bty at Toronto. Here's hoping I'll be a civilian again before another year. Spent today on battery duty with MacDougall. Have been reading *King Lear* with much enjoyment.

July 28, 1917   MacDougall and Shakespeare have continued to be my chief companions, both on and off duty. Enjoyed *A Midsummer Night's Dream*. Dunbar has gone down the line, suffering from "boils"—an uncommon malady among us here. May he make "Blighty" on it!

July 29, 1917   Back to the W.L. today for a brush-up course on telephone and visual signalling, with special attention to the newly introduced Fuller phone.

August 2, 1917 The cold, wet weather of the past few days is very reminiscent of last February and March and all too suggestive of the winter to come. Shall we be here for a fourth winter of war? News from Flanders reports a successful push along the Ypres front, in spite of bad weather.

August 6, 1917 Yesterday the sun came out and the mud shows signs of drying up. Today Don McLaren came over to see his brother Jack, which adds one more to the list of Orangeville boys met over here.

August 8, 1917 The Battery W.L. moved to a new location yesterday, all except the signallers. This afternoon we followed on horseback, through Souchez village and up the Souchez valley to Ablain-St. Nazaire of ancient memory. The rolling hills, so desolate with the rain and mud of early springtime when we toiled here on gun positions that are long since abandoned, make our surroundings now quite beautiful and well protected from cold winds. We slept in a hastily improvised lean-to of corrugated iron, thankful for this much shelter from a heavy night rain.

August 9, 1917 In spare moments today MacDougall and I built a very noble mansion and installed comfortable beds. Letter received from Dunbar, in England.

August 13, 1917 We have enjoyed very beautiful sunsets these past few evenings, in spite of rainy days. Our brush-up has been extended another week. Today I finished six months' service with the 9th Bty. How much longer, I wonder?

August 14, 1917　　Bun Aiken came over for a little visit this evening. He reported that Don McLaren is leaving shortly for his commission.

August 15, 1917　　The 1st and 2nd Division captured Hill 70 this morning, thus securing a commanding position by which to squeeze Fritz out of Lens. From our location here among the hills the noise of combat was subdued to a continuous low rumble of gunfire. News of victory reached us in the afternoon.

August 16, 1917　　Went for a walk through Carency and vicinity with Bun and Jack McLaren this evening.

August 21, 1917　　My course finished on the 19th and now I am up with the guns again. Seven months in France, as of yesterday, and still going strong. Lens is closely besieged by 1st, 2nd, and 4th Divisions. This fosse (mine shaft) is still a favourite target for Fritz's 4.1s.

August 26, 1917　　On Bde O.P. duty back on the crest with MacDougall today. Interesting but no sleep at night. Heavy rains. Artillery around Lens spasmodically active, making for us a brilliant display of fireworks like the Toronto Exhibition.

August 28, 1917　　Despite reports of mail lost, tonight brought a generous lot from Canada. Our work is rather disgustingly light these days and I am able to catch up in my correspondence. We shall be busy enough presently however. Fritz shoots quite a few at us daily, but with negligible results.

August 30, 1917   Letters from Ewart seem to indicate that he is receiving his first introduction to flying today, having transferred from the infantry to the R.F.C.

September 4, 1917   Taking advantage of entire freedom from duty and a gloriously fine day, I set out early for the "back country." After a sumptuous dinner at the W.L. (beans, Simcoe, 1 tin) I sallied boldly forth in search of brother Ross, with my gallant steed Reuben under me and Cpl. Bristow for company. A visit to Villers-au-Bois yielded no clue as to the P.P.'s whereabouts; but pressing on to Gouay-Servins, we found the entire battalion in billets there. However, I was doomed to disappointment for Ross had gone back to rest camp for ten days. The ride was certainly worthwhile anyway. The back country is quite delightful in the beauty of approaching harvest time and in its quiet peacefulness and almost entire freedom from the ugly scars of war. Another school year will be starting today. How many more will I miss?

September 5, 1917   Twice last night Fritz opened up a terrific bombardment on and around our position here with H.E. and gas shells. Luckily our gas curtain and our gas masks were in good condition and we suffered only from wakefulness. In another dug-out, however, MacDougall and Baillie were rather badly gassed and were sent down the line this evening. This afternoon Bdr. Fallas and I accompanied Lt. Vickery to our forward O.P. in Avion. Although we had overland line work to do en route (within sight of enemy positions) and spent several hours observing our artillery fire from a ruined school building some 300 yds. from the German front line, the afternoon passed without incident. More gas shells at night.

September 10, 1917 I learned that Ross visited our W.L. to see me today, so we have scored another miss. Fallas and I went forward on a 48-hr. liaison duty at noon.

September 12, 1917 Relieved on liaison by Wilkinson and Mills. The duty has been quite light and uneventful, but also almost sleepless. An unbroken stretch of fine weather so far this month.

September 15, 1917 Smith had to go down the line on Thurs. (13th) suffering from belated effects of gas. Am told that Ross made another unsuccessful attempt to see me at the W.L. yesterday.

September 17, 1917 Walked back to Mont St. Eloi this morning and spent the afternoon with Ross. Found him in good health and just preparing to go up the line for another turn in the trenches. I returned to the guns by way of the W.L. (still at Ablain-St. Nazaire) riding from there to the top of the Ridge by kindness of Colquhoun and two B.C. Party horses. A most enjoyable day!

September 20, 1917 Finished a 48-hour liaison duty with Capt. Magrath and J.R. Wilkinson. Smith returned from hospital today. Sgt. Henderson leaves for England on pass tomorrow, with Fallas taking temporary charge of the B.C. Party.

September 22, 1917 Am celebrating brother Art's birthday (with a lead of six hours on him) by a rather tedious battery duty with Wilkie. We have news of further advances by our troops at Ypres. A brilliant wind-up of the season's campaign here on our front seems to be in preparation. I wish it were safely over, for Ross will be in it on our right. Fritz will have to move fast to get clear of Lens before we coop him in.

September 29, 1917 Leaving the guns at 7 o'clock this morning, I walked the four or five miles to the W.L. and proceeded by horseback with Colquhoun to Hersin, most of the way across country. Returned by way of Aix-Noulette and Souchez and got back to the battery by 8 p.m. Hersin and vicinity look much more inviting in summer than in early spring. The open countryside is very beautiful and peaceful. Aix-Noulette remains badly battered, but the civilians seem to be coming back. The battlefront should be well out of range of those people before winter sets in. My French is poor but the word "oeuf" had not left me although it is a long time since I last partook of an egg. Assuredly the hen is a noble bird!

September 30, 1917 September has given us an absolutely perfect record of good weather. May October follow suit! Jimmie Fellows of the 9th Bty died of wounds tonight, just as his warrant for a ten-day Blighty leave came through.

October 2, 1917 Ross dropped in on his way down the line to go on leave. I walked back with him a little way towards the Ridge that has become so familiar a background during this summer campaign. It is too bad I could not have gone all the way with Ross to complete the reunion of the clan in England.

October 6, 1917   In the past two days the bright dry weather of September has ended and a cool west wind brings a touch of fall with it. Dame Rumour has been extremely busy for some time now, and today her whisperings are being suddenly substantiated. In a steady downpour of rain, which promises to continue indefinitely, orders have come to move our guns back to the W.L.; and from official sources there are dark references to a long march, the inference being Belgium. It seems that the Big Push up there is succeeding beyond all expectations and that the operations are to be extended to a degree not dreamed of a month ago. In this job the Canadian Corps is to participate instead of carrying on with the campaign here at Lens.

October 7, 1917   Came down to the W.L. with the Right Section late last night. Fortunately the rain had stopped but a very cold wind was blowing and I find that the sudden change has caught me unprepared. Today I wheeze, sniff and sneeze in turn and more rain has come to add to the discomfort. We switched back to solar time at one o'clock this morning.

October 8, 1917   Had a very enjoyable chat with Harry Vallentyne, my valued friend of Petawawa days, at noon today. He is with the 21st Bty so we should be reasonably near each other during the winter. Bad news of Mel Fydell, who is quite ill. A good hot bath at Carency this afternoon was much enjoyed, though it may not help my cold. Rumour persists that we are for Belgium very soon. It will be a long march, but a change of scenery.

October 11, 1917   Much rain and mud but my cold is improving. Have spent a couple of evenings with Val and was over to see Bun and Don McLaren on Tuesday. We move north tomorrow.

MARCH TO BELGIUM

October 12, 1917   Here we are at Annezin, a suburb of Béthune, prepared to spend the night in a fairly comfortable shack reserved for us by the billeting party. The march has been a hard one for our unaccustomed feet. This morning the weather cleared, following a night of continuous rain; but in the afternoon we marched through rain and mud. Our way led by a roundabout way through Gouay-Servins, Grand-Servins, Coupigny, Hersin and Noeux-les-Mines: totaling some 23 kilometres.

October 13, 1917   Rain and sunshine have alternated many times over while we trudged on another 20 kilometres through Robecq and St. Vennat to our next stopping place here in Mobecque. Mud is not proving any great hindrance to our progress, for the roads are good and well drained. But the cobblestones with which most of the roads are paved make for bruised feet among the "Foot Guards." We seem to have left behind the coal-mining regions and are now passing through farming country, well wooded and prosperous looking. The houses, both in town and country, are tile-roofed or thatched, never roofed with cedar shingles. Individual farm buildings seem of more frequent occurrence here than farther south, where the old French custom of village residences for farmers seems to obtain quite generally. An occasional water-wheel and many windmills are in evidence. Tonight I spent two hours on picket duty, then settled down comfortably on bales of hay for the remaining hours of darkness.

October 14, 1917   A bright sunshiny day followed the heavy rains of last night and we set out on the road once more with high spirits and healthy appetites. By 11 o'clock we were passing through Hazebroucke, a town of considerable size but cloaked with a Sunday quietness rudely broken by the endless convoys of military supplies and personnel passing along its main streets. Here I had the good fortune to meet Jimmie Collins, a sergeant in the 4th C.M.R.s. A road through a considerable forest brought us to St. Sylvestre-Cappel, thence through Steenvoorde to a farm billet between Ecke and Godwersville. My feet are still bothering me, probably because of ill-fitting boots, and I was glad when we reached the end of our 17-kilometre march. We slept very comfortably in a shed next door to a friendly young calf, after indulging in some very refreshing milk kindly provided by the farmer's wife. My French is improving slightly; wish I had more practice.

October 15, 1917   Our hopes of resting here a day or two were rudely interrupted by an early reveille, and soon we were again ready for the road. I had the pleasure of a brief chat with Earl Stevenson, who was riding past us with the advance party of the 33rd Bty; received reassuring news of other chaps from Orangeville. We crossed over into Belgium before noon and passing through Abeele, Poperinghe, Brandhoek and Vlamertinghe, we came at last to our new home, for how long no one knows. Our W.L. are established among the ruins of an old asylum on the western outskirts of Ypres and we are to sleep for tonight just anywhere we can lay our weary heads. Our march today covered some 20 kilometres. The weather has been fine and we are able to ride the limbers part of the way. The four-day trip has totalled some 80 kilometres (50 miles) in length.

October 16, 1917   The Battery went into action today, taking over the four guns left by the British battery we are relieving. I have been left behind with the W.L. detachment but shall doubtless soon have a turn forward. There is evidently plenty of work ahead here at the W.L. getting settled in this old group of buildings, long since converted to wartime uses. It has been raining today at intervals.

October 17, 1917   Everybody busy on horse lines and billets. Good weather has returned, fortunately. Apparently this is an extremely active front: much bombing and shelling by Fritz even away back here. Endless traffic on the roads, day and night.

October 18, 1917   Our happy home leaked last night, badly; so today we laboured arduously on the roof. Our position aloft was rather an unsteady one, for most of the spare gunners and drivers organized themselves into a wrecking crew and proceeded to pull down walls quite indiscriminately here and there, not sparing our feelings in the least. However, the job was accomplished in expert fashion and now our home is comfortably established. Already our casualties total six: one killed (Shearer) five wounded. Bombs accounted for two and shells for the rest. It is a decidedly hot spot at the guns. I saw several big Gotha bombing planes doing their destructive work not far away today, and we hear them nightly overhead. But I guess we are not taking all this punishment without reason and without good return.

October 19, 1917   The sad news reached us this evening that Colquhoun has been killed and Dobbin wounded, besides two more casualties among the gunners. MacDougall, L.T. Wilkinson and I are to go up to the guns with Cpl. Bristow in the early morning. Two more signallers have been added to our number to date: O'Brien and D'Arcy. Must get a letter off home before I leave.

October 20, 1917   For my travelling companions and myself reveille came very early this morning: two o'clock, forsooth! A detachment of drivers left at 3 a.m. for a packing trip, so we rode on their off-horses through Ypres and along the Zonnebeke road as far as the ammunition dump. Dismounting there we walked the rest of the distance to the guns, arriving just before dawn. We were greeted by the news that Sgt. Henderson was also wounded yesterday, though not seriously; so our signal staff has been badly depleted. The coming of dawn disclosed a most desolate scene. The entire expanse of country in all directions is one unbroken waste, unspeakably dreary and barren. Shell-hole merged into shell-hole, all water-filled and well nigh impassable at any point. The road nearby is terribly cut and lined on both sides with all the litter of recent battle; it is remarkable how it supports the continuous flow of traffic that passes along it both day and night. There are no proper dug-outs, for such are impossible in this wet soil. The gunners are living in a makeshift shelter in an old culvert under the railway embankment. The officers and signallers are living in splinter-proof (nearly) but not shell-proof shelters built into enlarged shell-holes near the guns. A plank floor covers the watery bottom and it is a regular duty of the signallers to bail out the overflow lest we be submerged. Fritz shells all this area almost incessantly and our artillery replies in like measure. Line breaks are frequent and nearly always mended under shellfire. Wilkie and I were detailed for battery duty, so our sleep will be limited again tonight. Nine months' active service in France and Belgium completed.

October 21, 1917   Communications were maintained without interruption all night, so our duty period passed off uneventfully except for the deluge of shells that fell about us at intervals. Not much work to do today except to lie low and dodge such shells as became rather too "familiar."

Two more drivers were wounded this morning, totalling twelve since coming to this front, and two guns were knocked out this afternoon; but these present difficulties are merely a phase of the operations in progress and when we have captured the remaining objectives things will be much better.

October 22, 1917   On duty at the battery alone most of the day, for Bristow and the rest went forward on other work. I guess this is the hottest corner the 9th Battery has been in for many months, certainly since I joined it. We are evidently in the middle of a large square of territory on which Fritz has his guns all nicely registered, and intermittently day and night he searches up and down its area with his shells. More than once he had me beautifully ringed about with fast 4.1s while he deliberately proceeded to cut up my telephone lines outside the circle. It was not a particularly pleasant job mending them, but he hit neither me nor my shell-hole home and I have no complaint coming. Strange how disinterested one can remain, so long as he is on duty and busy, even though at any time a shell might fall through the roof and cause considerable disorder within! Early this morning our guns on the whole front opened a barrage the strength of which surely promises well for our next attack. The heavies continued to strafe during most of the day.

October 23, 1917   A night duty ended without incident and early morning brought our relief a day sooner than expected in the persons of J.R. Wilkinson and Black. L.T. Wilkinson and

I left for the W.L. about 11:00 and boarded the first lorry passing in our direction. It was a rough passage and only with difficulty did we remain on board. Outside of Ypres we disembarked by mutual consent and proceeded on foot through the Menin Gate (hardly discernible now) and along the main thoroughfares of this old battered town to our home on the Poperinghe road. On the way I chanced to see a P.P. man, so in the afternoon I set forth in search of Ross. Found him without much trouble and spent an enjoyable couple of hours with him. He looks well, but I cannot restrain a dread of the dangerous operations in which he will soon be engaged. The same protecting Hand still rules over our destinies, however, so fear is unjustified.

October 24, 1917   A day of peace and comfort; washing and drying myself and my clothes, writing letters, sleeping, etc. Bright weather and an optimistic feeling. French successes reported from the south. A note from Ross informed me that he is still "in town" so I went over and had dinner with him. He expects to go forward tomorrow.

October 25, 1917   Another pleasant surprise! Ross called around this evening to tell me that he will be near me for another day or two. So we went for a walk through Ypres, visiting the ruins of the Cathedral and the Cloth Hall and proceeding out to the Lille Gate. There the ramparts and moat still remain, though the walls are badly battered. I returned with Ross to his quarters and left him there with a promise to see him again tomorrow afternoon.

THE BATTLE OF PASSCHENDAELE

October 26, 1917   Early this morning our infantry (3rd and 4th Divisions) went over the top in the first phase of the battle for Passchendaele Ridge. Rain and mud impeded the advance but all or nearly all objectives are reported taken. The 58th Bn was held up until afternoon by some "pillboxes" (concrete emplacements). Prisoners kept dribbling through Ypres all day. Spent the evening again with Ross, staying for dinner at the company mess. Served a two-hour picket duty at night. Parcel received from Marjorie Richardson, after sharing one recently received from her by Ross.

October 27, 1917   Lost the toss with L.T. Wilkinson to go up to the guns this morning; but was quite content to stay, for this evening again I spent an hour with Ross. He goes forward tomorrow evening; I go up in the early morning. May we both be kept safely through the strenuous experiences ahead of us!

October 28, 1917   Up to the guns again this morning, most of the way by motor lorry. Our battery position was very heavily shelled for two or three hours around noon, but our heavies are doubtless making Fritz hop about on the other side of the ridge.

October 29, 1917   We were shelled heavily again this morning and at noon. The Bde line was cut and Wilkie (L.T.) and I sallied forth to repair the damage. Our work was all but completed when two shells in quick succession fell nearly on top of us. Both of us were blown into a shell-hole and almost mired. I soon found that poor Wilkie had suffered severe wounds to the left wrist and right thigh. Bristow and Unwin were soon on the spot and we carried him over to Pill-Box V, where Capt. Steele of the 12th Bty helped us to give first aid and later to carry him down the road to the nearest dressing station. Unwin and I went back on the line to reopen communications. We are hoping that with immediate attention Wilkie will be O.K. My own escape was miraculous. In the afternoon orders arrived for Bristow, MacDougall and me to go forward with Lt. Macpherson on liaison duty for the coming attack. Two men from other batteries in our Bde accompanied us, leaving about 4 p.m. and arriving at 85th Bn HQ two hours later. Fortunately, the weather is good and Fritz is quiet so we have been able to align our lamps and complete all other necessary preparations. HQ is in a pill-box about 300 yds in rear of our present front lines. Fritz is some 50 yds farther away. We did not lay any wire, for it would not remain unbroken once the scrap begins. Lamp or runner will be the medium back to Report Centre, thence by buried cable to Artillery Bde HQ.

October 30, 1917   The night was cold and my discomfort was increased by being wet to the knees from my experience with Wilkie. But there is an end to everything. In the early morning Bristow left me alone at "Hillside Farm" and went back to where MacDougall and the others awaited such messages as my lamp might blink to them. Then began the storm of our barrage; guns and machine guns, from as far back as Ypres, opened up at 5:45 a.m. with a fearful hail of missiles. Fritz's come-back was prompt and heavy and soon the crashing of his shells was added to the roar of our own guns. Naturally, the forward pill-boxes in our possession were given lots of attention in the enemy's counter-barrage and my location, even on the lee-side of Bn HQ, was not a comfortable one. However, the necessary messages went through all right—for a while. Before long, prisoners and our own wounded men began to arrive on their way back from the fighting front and several took refuge beside me against the wall of the pill-box.

Then hostile planes appeared above us, dropping bombs, and our doom seemed to be sealed. The nearest bomb fell with deadly effect, its fragments killing seven of those crouching beside me. Three of us only were left, dazed but full of gratitude for our deliverance. I thought for a moment that my face had been badly torn, so great was the concussion as it swept by me; but only a minute particle hit me, lodging at the outer edge of my eye. I could no longer pick up any trace of the distant lamp, though I called persistently with mine; and I feared greatly for the safety of my comrades. To my intense relief, however, Bristow and King (10th Bty) came along about noon and we retired into the pill-box, thereafter carrying messages by hand back to Report Centre, communication by lamp having proved no longer possible. All reports from forward indicated all objectives attained and held, but the 85th Bn paid a heavy price in casualties and supporting companies of the 38th were called up. Far into the afternoon the artillery on both sides continued the fight; but Fritz made no counter-attack on our front and gradually the noise of battle subsided.

October 31, 1917   Early this morning King and I went back with despatches and remained for a few hours' rest at a forward O.P. near Report Centre. Our work seems to be nearly finished but we have not yet been relieved and have evidently another night here ahead of us. The situation has been fairly normal through the day and such trips as we had, back and forth, have been comparatively unexciting. This evening, however, the artillery has stirred things up again and it is nowhere very healthful.

November 1, 1917   Spent a part of last night at the forward O.P. again and passed safely through a heavy air attack including gas bombs. This morning was fairly quiet and this afternoon we were relieved after a 72-hour duty. We stopped at the guns for supper and then continued to the W.L. There found to my great relief that Ross had also passed through the fighting unhurt; I missed seeing him by just a few minutes. We have both reason for the deepest gratitude to God for our deliverance and safekeeping. Another old member of our B.C. Party, Alf Mills, was killed by a bomb dropped on the W.L. just last night. Alf came out as trumpeter with the original 9th Bty and was a very courageous soldier, cheerful and helpful under all circumstances.

November 2, 1917   A good hot bath and a sound night's sleep have made me feel quite fit again. Today I saw Lester Arnott, who is attached to the 9th Bty from the D.A.C. for packing ammunition.

Mills was buried today beside Colquhoun in the cemetery on the Dickebusch road.

November 3, 1917   My rest this time has been short. At 1:30 a.m I was wakened to go up to the guns again with Black and Unwin. We are short-handed now, for Mason and McClennan are on leave and Smith is ready to go on leave, and the signallers have suffered six casualties in this position. This total includes a chap named Seymans who joined us, along with another new man (Vale), and was up at the guns only a few hours before being wounded. Our trip up was quieter than usual, but there is still much strafing here. With Fallas and O'Brien I spent most of the day stringing a new line to the O.P. but visibility was not good enough to register the three guns that have come back from Ordnance (in addition to the two still in action). Seymans died of his wounds.

November 5, 1917   Promotions announced today include Sgt. Bristow, Cpl. Fallas and Bdr. Wilkinson of the B.C. Party and Bdr. Cameron among the gunners: all timely and well deserved. At noon today a relief came up so Vale and I journeyed back to our "asylum" for another little rest.

November 6, 1917   Early this morning the 1st and 2nd Canadian Divisions went over the top and, by all reports, have established the line well over Passchendaele Ridge. The rain has kept off marvellously during our operations here, though the past few days have been dull. A new draft from the D.A.C. today brought us three more signallers (Butt, Mayhew, and Lamb); these, with McDonald, who joined us yesterday, bring our total to one more than we had on arrival at Ypres. What a long and eventful three weeks it has been!

November 7, 1917   Got off for a holiday today and Lester Arnott and I journeyed by motor lorry to Poperinghe for a few hours. There, in the old Military Cemetery on Reninghelst Road, we found Harry McGuire's grave, a quiet resting place among the other heroes (French, British, and Canadian) of the dark days of April 1915. It is sacred ground and with reverence we read each simple inscription. Lt. Col. Boyle, Lt. Col. Hart-McHarg and other familiar names are there that will live in the history of the Second Battle of Ypres; one 9th Bty man's name I saw was that of Lovekin.

We dined on pork chops and chips and custard pie, and spent an hour at the movies before setting out on our return journey. Sent a note to Ross by kindness of a P.P. man whom I chanced to see.

November 8, 1917   Fifty casualties to date, exclusive of light cases returned to the Battery. There are so many new men among us now that it seems almost a strange unit. Rumour has it that we are to move soon, back for rest or to another front. The considerable amount of gas inhaled the past week up

the line has given me a bad cough. Cpl. Fallas was officially decorated with the M.M. today.

November 10, 1917   Came up to the guns again early this morning
with Vale. Miserable weather now but we should be away
from here soon. Cough still bothersome. Cpl. Fallas went
on pass today. This evening I had to go up to the O.P. to
straighten out some difficulties two of the new chaps had
encountered, and stayed through a wet cold night. Met Orr
and Drybrough, 67th Bty men.

November 11, 1917   An R.F.A. battery took over our position and
guns late this afternoon, so here we are back at the W.L.
again. Fritz treated us to a salvo of "close ones" just before
we left, so we are not at all sorry to get away from the old
"boat." Nobody knows just where we go next, but we start
for there in a day or two.

November 13, 1917   On the road once more and everybody
happy! The column pulled out of our asylum home and
soon after 8:00 this morning, passed through
Vlamertinghe and skirted around the south of
Poperinghe, thence to Abeele and then over the border to
Godewaersvaele, Ecke and Caestre. We parked our guns
and limbers in a field to the west of Caestre and slept
nearby in tents, crowded but warm. So far I am traveling
on foot again, but my feet are in good shape and I feel no
ill effects of our 28-kilometre march. Passing through
Vlamertinghe, I had the good fortune to see Ross with his
company proceeding up the line in motor lorries and had

The band of the 36th Regiment, at Niagara Camp, June 15 to 26, 1909. From left to right: Top Row: H. Webster, G. Brets, Dixie, Prof. Laugher, Dixon, R. Morrow, Bowler, E. Hall, J. Cameron, P. Harding, Tapping. Middle Row: M. Webster, W. Patterson, H. Galbraith, T.F.E. Claridge, A. Matthews, J. Crago, L. Hall. Front Row: Donald S. Macpherson, M. Sawyers, McLean.

High school cadets in Orangeville, Ontario, May 31, 1912.
Donald Macpherson is in the centre.

The 67th Battery, C.F.A., C.E.F., University Battery, Toronto, circa 1916.

The 67th Battery at Petawawa, 1916.

A portrait of Donald Macpherson, soon after enlistment in the 67th Battery, Toronto, July 1916.

The Signalling class at Petawawa, August, 1916.

Donald Macpherson in
training at Petawawa,
September 16, 1916.

This hut is similar to the one in which Donald Macpherson stayed while in training at Shorncliffe Camp near Folkestone, winter 1916-17.

TIN TOWN, SHORNCLIFFE CAMP

Excerpts from Lt. Macpherson's War Diaries.

Wednesday, October 4

277 days past   88 to come

The list of the men detailed for the coming overseas draft was posted today. As expected, I am on it, as are practically all my friends in the Battery except Val, who is to be QMS, and Neil who intends taking the course at Kingston within a month from now, we shall ~~hostility~~ to be on the "briny deep".

This Book contains the Diary of

Name *Donald S. Macpherson*

Rank and Number *Gunner #337976*

Battalion, Battery, etc. *67th (Varsity) Battery*
                                  C.F.A.

Brigade *A*

Date of enlistment *July 14th, 1916*

Where enlisted *Toronto, Ont.*

Should this book be found,
kindly forward it to the undersigned.

To you these writings may not mean much,
To others they mean everything that's dear.

THANK YOU!

Name *Mrs. D. Macpherson*

Address *Orangeville, Ont.*

(Box 271)   Canada

The call to service overseas.

Title page of the first diary.

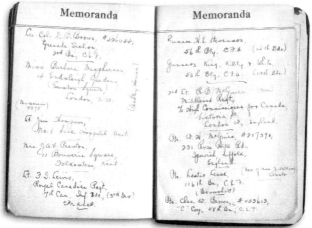

Lists of names and addresses of fellow servicemen.

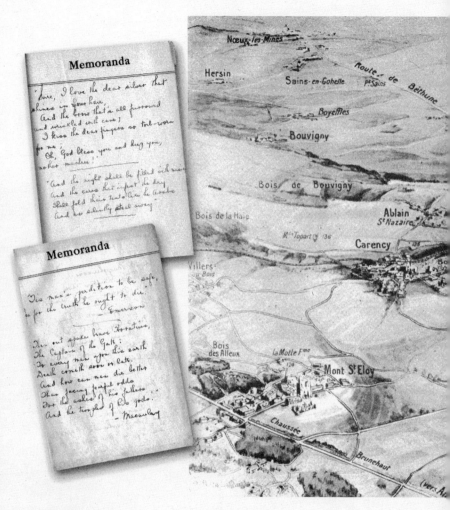

Memoranda

hure, I love the dear silver that
shines in your hair,
And the brows that's all furrowed
and wrinkled with care;
I kiss the dear fingers so toil-worn
for me,
Oh, God bless you and keep you,
mother machree!

"And the night shall be filled with music
And the cares that infest the day
Shall fold their tents like the arabs
And as silently steal away.

Memoranda

'Tis man's perdition to be safe,
When for the truth he ought to die.
— Emerson

Then out spake brave Horatius,
The Captain of the Gate:
To every man upon this earth
Death cometh soon or late.
And how can man die better
Than facing fearful odds
For the ashes of his fathers
And the temples of his gods.
— Macaulay

Scraps of verse Donald
Macpherson found
meaningful.

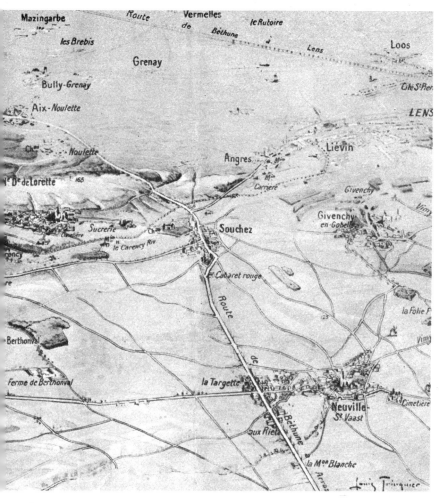

A French map of the countryside north of Arras, showing a number of places mentioned in the diary: Loos, Notre Dame de Lorette, Souchez, Neuville St. Vaast, Ablain St. Nazaire, Mont St. Eloy. From *The Illustrated War News*, June 2, 1915.

"Trench Map, France, Sheet 36C S.W.", showing the Vimy Ridge area. Lt. Macpherson has marked the location of the Canadian Monument at Hill 145, and the locations of the 9th Battery outside Vimy, from May 7 to June 4, 1917.

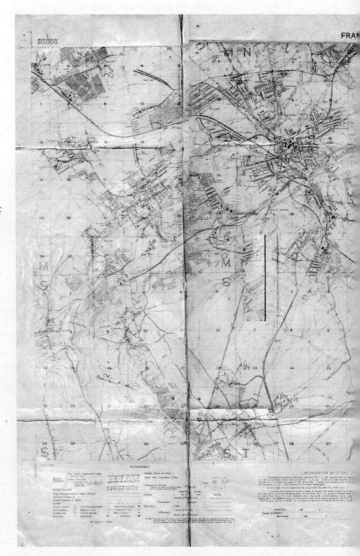

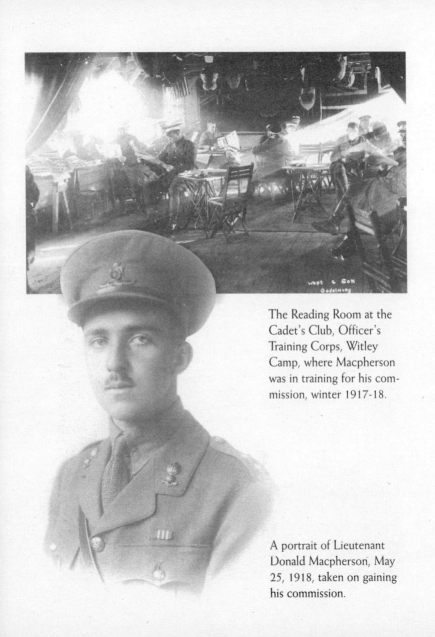

The Reading Room at the Cadet's Club, Officer's Training Corps, Witley Camp, where Macpherson was in training for his commission, winter 1917-18.

A portrait of Lieutenant Donald Macpherson, May 25, 1918, taken on gaining his commission.

Cadet Macpherson in training for Commission, Witley Camp, England, February 5th, 1918.

The distinguished Macpherson soldier brothers, together for New Years Eve in London England, December 31, 1917.

Back row: left, Donald S. Macpherson, Gunner, 67th (Varsity) Battery, C.E.F.; centre, Ewart G. Macpherson, Royal Flying Corps; right, Uncle Arthur Willson. Front row left, J. Ross Macpherson, Princess Patricia's Light Infantry and Douglas W. Macpherson, 16th Canadian Scottish Regiment. The youngest Macpherson brother, Arthur (not present here), later served in the RCAF in the Second World War as a chaplain.

An illustration showing the Macpherson brothers, from *Canada in the Great World War* (United Publishing of Canada Ltd, 1921).

LIEUT. DONALD S. MACPHERSON, M.M.

CAPT. J. ROSS MACPHERSON, D.S.O. Killed in action, August 26th, 1918

LIEUT. EWART G. MACPHERSON

LIEUT. DOUGLAS W. MACPHERSON, M.C.

SOLDIER BROTHERS

The war memorial erected at Orangeville high school after the war to honour students who gave their lives for their country.

just time for a few words with him. Disappointed to learn that he is to have another three days forward on the front. I passed Alex Fleming farther down the street but had no time to speak to him.

November 14, 1917   This morning I sallied bravely forth, along with the "miscellaneous" that follows in rear of a column on the march, mounted bareback on a disreputable looking mule that had been picked up and wished on the B.C. Party. But passing through Hazebroucke, alas, my charger was taken from me and harnessed to the mess cart in place of one which had become lame. So I had, perforce, to resume my place among the "gravel crushers." However, 15 kilometres was the limit of our day's journey and, after passing through Morbecque, we stopped in Steenbecque, billeted for a night this time on the straw of a comfortable shed.

November 15, 1917   A change in routine orders for today placed Unwin and me in the billeting party in place of Black and MacDougall; so the early dawn found us riding quickly in the direction of our next stopping place, which we found to be Millinghem. The finding and allotting of billets for a whole brigade of artillery is rather a big job, but everything was well arranged by the time the head of our column arrived at the outskirts of the town. Once more a shed is our "boudoir" with thick clean straw to sleep on.

November 16, 1917   The glorious weather which has attended each day's journey thus far still continues. It is a real pleasure to ride forth in the early morning through a quiet, peaceful countryside, far from Fritz's shells and the sound of guns. Today our route lay through Lillers, Lozinghen and Marles-les-Mines down into quiet little Lapugnoy, where again we spent a busy time locating lines and billets for the brigade. One of the officers in the party today was Plaskett, formerly of the 67th Bty and now attached to the 10th. MacDougall has gone on leave; Johnson has become a casualty, suffering from ill-effects of gas.

November 17, 1917   Another change in our schedule! Orders came along late last evening that we are to take over gun positions sooner than expected. This morning Mason and I accompanied Lt. Raynor on foot back to Marles-les-Mines, where we joined a similar party from the 10th and 12th Batteries and boarded a motor lorry going south. Through Bruay, Houdain, Gauchin-Legal (where we saw our billeting party already at work for the night's spot), Camblain l'Abbé, Mont St. Eloi and Neuville-St. Vaast we sped in a short two hours' ride and finally disembarked at Thélus crossroads. Back home again to the land of trenches and deep dug-outs! It was almost like a dream after the horrible realities of the Belgian battlefront, now far behind us to the north. Guides awaited us and we were led to a position just two hundred yards in advance of the former La Chaudière "home." It is a good position and most restfully quiet. Our Battery takes over tomorrow.

November 18, 1917   Spent a busy morning checking over the various telephone lines and locating Bde HQ, O.P., etc. At noon Major Cook and two gun crews arrived, and our Imperial friends of the D140 Battery left (they think) for a long trip to Italy. They are a sorry lot to have to leave this comfortable location.

November 20, 1917   Sgt. Bristow came up with two men, so Lamb and I trudged through the mud to the W.L. this evening. We found the W.L. located on the Arras-Béthune road, just at the foot of the plank road leading forward to Givenchy. We learn with deep sorrow that L.T. Wilkinson died of the wounds he received on October 29. In him we have lost another good comrade and a courageous soldier.

November 21, 1917   My rest proved a short one. Vale is decidedly under the weather and could not take his regular turn forward. So Butt and I accompanied two guns and their crews that have been suddenly ordered into action here in an old 35th Bty position just north of Vimy Station. A narrow-gauge railway transported the entire outfit, with considerable ammunition, almost the whole distance from La Targette. The guns will be man-handled into the pits in the early morning; meantime we are resting for the night in the depths of a dug-out under the railway embankment. It is officially reported that we have made a break in the enemy's line down Bapaume way, and all available infantry and artillery have been hastily withdrawn from this front to make the most of the situation there. Hence the necessity of our operating two battery positions.

November 23, 1917   Butt has returned to the W.L. in search of a dentist, so MacDougall is here with me now. The guns were registered today. Fair weather but colder.

November 24, 1917   Ordered to report to Col. MacDonald at Bde HQ this morning. Spent the time en route conjecturing as to whether the summons meant a V.C. or a court martial; but to my intense surprise I found that I had been recommended, along with Sgt. Lister and Sgt. Brown, for a commission! The Colonel appeared to receive me favourably and we have now to go before the Divisional Commander. Whatever inspired Major Cook (O.C. 9th Bty) to do this for me I cannot say; but I am glad that my chance has come to gratify this ambitious spirit of mine, and now that the matter has progressed this far, joy be the consequence! Sixteen months in the army today; ten months in France and Belgium; number eleven on the pass list for Blighty and prospects of a four-months' sojourn there on course instead. Black has been taken off strength as a prospective orderly room clerk.

November 25, 1917   First snowfall of the season today. Met Alf Warman (2nd Pioneers) this morning, just outside our gun position.

November 27, 1917   Sgt. Lister is to proceed to England at an early date, but Sgt. Brown and I will probably have to wait for a month or so for the next time. All three applications have evidently been received by Division. Now I shall have to decide whether to take my leave when it comes or wait for my commission course to start.

November 28, 1917   In compliance with a message that arrived late last night I rode back to 4th Division HQ at the Chateau D'Acq this afternoon and reported for interview with Gen. King. Result not entirely satisfactory, because I lacked the apparently necessary certificate of education and character. I was told to procure these at the earliest possible date; in the meantime it looks as though I may have missed an opportunity to go on course almost immediately. Lt. Macpherson (9th Bty) seems to think that he can arrange with the staff captain to waive these requirements, but I doubt if he can.

November 29, 1917   Back on my old job of advance party expert! About midnight I was wakened from a sound sleep and told to be ready to leave with Lt. Kennedy at 9 a.m. for the brigade is moving out for rest tomorrow. So here we are at Haillicourt after a long ride via Souchez, Ablain l'Abbé Petit and Gouay Servins, and Barlin. Here or hereabouts will be the brigade's stopping place for its three weeks' rest.

November 30, 1917   Have had a busy day with Lt. Kennedy procuring suitable horse lines and billets for the 9th Bty and for the Bde HQ. This is a most unsatisfactory place for a lengthy stay; open standings and very ordinary billets. The column arrived between 3 and 4 o'clock in the afternoon and I was very busily engaged until long after dark showing everybody where everything is located. Good weather but cold.

December 1, 1917   Spent the day straightening out billeting difficulties and drawing a very elaborate (and artistic!) plan,
which might be entitled "Where's What?", as its purpose is
to show everyone concerned just where all personnel, horses, harnesses, equipment, etc. of the Battery and Bde HQ
are to be found.

December 2, 1917   Armed with a pass from my namesake officer (Lt.
Macpherson) and mounted on "Miss Vickery" I went on a
long journey this morning in search of certain certificates
aforementioned. Riding through Barlin, Hersin, Boyeffles,
Aix-Noulette and Souchez, I finally arrived in Ablain-St.
Nazaire where I found the 1st and 2nd Bde located.
Fortunately, Gerald Preston was at home and he very kindly
gave me a written certificate of good character based on our
ten years' acquaintanceship. Luckily he did not hesitate to
strain his conscience a bit. Proceeding to the W.L. we had
vacated just last Friday, I found Jack Newton of the 22nd Bty
and he gave me the required certificate as to education. It
was a long ride and I did not get back to our present lines
here until 5:30 p.m. Found Dunbar (now of the 45th Bty)
paying the gang a visit, looking well and hearty after his "holiday" in hospital. Bristow and Wilkinson went on leave today.
I am now No. 2 on the Battery list for Blighty. A letter came
in the mail from Ross at St. Hilaire, the first word I have had
from him since seeing him at Vlamertinghe on November 13.

December 3, 1917   Walked in to Bruay this afternoon and presented my application for commission, with certificates

attached, to Staff Captain Savage at 4th Division Artillery HQ. I was told that I shall have to interview Gen. Morrison presently and that I shall probably not be proceeding to England with the very next class to leave from here, so I guess I'll take my pass when it comes along and spend Christmas in old England, or Scotland. A letter from Doug brings the news that he is still in England but now ready for an early draft back to the 16th Bn. Weather still bright but quite cold with hard frosts at night.

December 4, 1917   Sgt. Lister left for England today with several others from our Brigade. My turn may come with the next lot to go.

December 7, 1917   Mounted inspection of the whole Brigade this afternoon by Major Cook, acting Col.: probably a prelude to a general inspection later on. MacDougall has returned from leave. On picket duty tonight as a punishment for lateness on afternoon parade! Weather moderating with some rain.

December 8, 1917   Black and Unwin and Burns departed on leave for Blighty this morning. My turn next week, probably. Weather bright and moderately warm.

AWARDED THE MILITARY MEDAL

December 9, 1917   Church parade and communion service this morning; all too infrequent a privilege in this land of war. At noon Pete Welford of Bde brought me the astounding news that I have been awarded the Military Medal, what for remains to be explained! I am not conscious of having done anything except whatever duty happened to come to me from time to time during the difficult days at Ypres; and all our men did the same. If it is intended as an honour to the B.C. Party in general, it is well deserved. I hope someone else has also been chosen for decoration.

December 10, 1917   In accordance with instructions brought to me about midnight, rode forth early this morning to keep an appointment with Gen. Morrison, the G.O.C.R.A. (General Officer Commanding Royal Artillery) Canadian Corps. The way led through Barlin, Hersin, Coupigny, Grand Servins and on to Camblain-l'Abbé, my final objective, which I reached just in time at 8:30 a.m. Men from all the various brigades in the Corps were there, to the number of some twenty in all, and each in turn was called in for a brief interview with the General. I learned to my dismay that Division had not forwarded my papers in time but the General very kindly intimated that he would be pleased to recommend me, just as soon as my papers reached him, without requiring another visit. This leaves the matter in a reasonably satisfactory state. Meantime, I shall take my leave when it comes and keep my date with Doug and Ewart for Christmas Day.

A part of the Battery voted this afternoon and my ballot went in for the Union Government.

I learn that Unwin also had been awarded the M.M. and Bristow has received a Bar to his former decoration, so I have some company in my sudden and unexpected notoriety. Sgt. Lister and Bdr. Nichols have been likewise honoured.

December 12, 1917   Ross rode over to see me today, arriving about noon. He had lunch with the officers of the Battery and in the afternoon we rode into Béthune together to do a little shopping, including my M.M. ribbon. Ross came back with me to Haillicourt and then rode on to Bruay for the night. He looks well and fit and speaks hopefully of a furlough home to Canada this winter. Sgt. Henderson returned to the Battery this afternoon.

December 13, 1917   The Battery went for a route march through Bruay and back this morning to the music of a band. Quite a pleasant change from the usual drab routine.

December 14, 1917   The Brigade was inspected this afternoon by Gen. King, 4th Division O.C. Am disappointed again about my pass; the Adjutant thinks I had better wait in case orders come through to proceed on my course for a commission.

December 15, 1917   The Brigade will go back into action within a few days, so tonight our Battery held its Christmas dinner in the town school-house, which was suitably decorated for the occasion. Roast goose, with mashed potatoes and other trimmings, followed by a generous piece of mince pie and accompanied by a moderate portion of French beer for those who wished it made up the main part of the feast. Well-filled Christmas stockings from Mrs. Ross of Toronto were distributed, along with socks, towels and cigarettes from other sources. About midway through the dinner Lt. Kennedy informed me that I would be leaving for England in the morning, so much of the night was spent in hurried preparations for this sudden move.

TO ENGLAND ON COURSE

December 16, 1917   Spent most of this morning in repeated visits to Bde for the various documents necessary for my trip to Blighty and in hasty leave takings with various friends. It is hard to leave a unit after ten months of active campaigning; one quickly makes good friends in the army. Eleven months in France, including D.A.C.

Mason rode down to Béthune with me, where I entrained at one o'clock. A six-hour run via Lillers and St. Omer brought the train with its merry load of men going on leave to Boulogne, our port of departure. There we marched to a roomy and comfortable rest billet to spend the night. The weather is cold, with snow.

December 17, 1917   Men proceeding on duty (not on leave) were withheld from the first boat leaving today and it was not until 3 p.m. that we steamed out of harbour, bound for "dear old Blighty." The passage was cold, rough and wet (by reason of the spray which a strong head-wind continually blew in on us); all on board were very glad when we docked at Folkestone Harbour after nearly a two-hour trip. Instead of boarding one of the leave trains that awaited us, I walked up to the Royal Pavilion Hotel and phoned to Doug, who came down from camp later and spent the evening with me. It was a happy reunion after our separation of eleven months. Now to connect up with Ewart!

December 18, 1917   Was wakened out of a comfortable sleep this morning just in time to catch the 8:20 London train at Central Station. Reached Cannon Street Station at 10:15 and proceeded to Argyle House on Regent Street (Can. HQ). There I received instructions to report at Witley Camp; so I caught the 2:55 p.m. train at Waterloo Station and here I am for the night. I expect to go on leave tomorrow, so shall be free for both Christmas and New Year's Day. Weather continues quite frosty, with considerable snow on the ground.

December 19, 1917   Back in London again, by the 11:43 train from Milford this morning. Have taken temporary residence in the Maple Leaf Club in Connaught Place and am trying to get in touch with Ewart. Weather very cold last night and now a heavy fog hangs over the "Big Smoke." It is just eleven months ago tonight since I landed at Le Havre. I have been fortunate to get back on course so soon.

December 20, 1917   Ran across Black (9th Bty) at breakfast this morning and found that he had slept in the next room to mine last night. This afternoon we went together to see "Round the Map" at the Alhambra Theatre: a fairly entertaining show. Black is off to another show tonight, but one in a day is enough for me.

December 21, 1917   A trip to the Pay Office netted me £14 this morning. A visit to Gamage's this afternoon relieved me of £3 for boots, puttees and spurs. Sent a cable home tonight conveying Christmas greetings and request for £10 of my deferred pay. It is going to require money to be even a Cadet! Have arranged a trip to Pewsey to see Ewart tomorrow.

December 22, 1917   Ewart met me at Pewsey Station at noon today and after lunch in the village we proceeded to the Flying School (5 miles away) by R.F.C. mail tender. Capt. Wilberforce, Flight Commander, very kindly took me up for a 15-minute flight; an interesting and enjoyable experience. Later I watched Ewart do a short solo flight; evidently he has pretty well mastered the intricacies of flying and is well past the worst stages of the training process.

December 23, 1917   Slept comfortably in Ewart's quarters last night and woke to another bright, frosty day; beautiful Christmas weather down here in Wiltshire, with considerable snow on the ground. Ewart went up for about an hour this morning. In the afternoon we walked to Pewsey and had supper together at a pleasant little village inn, after which I caught the 6:38 train for London and proceeded immediately towards Glasgow by the 11:30 train from Euston Station.

December 24, 1917   This is written at 53 Dixon Ave, where I have been most heartily welcomed by my Glasgow cousins. Barbara and Mary had a half-holiday from school and escorted me downtown in the afternoon to Moore & Taggarts, where I placed an order for my cadet uniform while they made other purchases. I have met also Agnes, as well as Mr. and Mrs. Macpherson; all the boys are away soldiering or on other national services. They are a jolly family and "the soul of hospitality;" one feels immediately at home in their midst.

December 25, 1917   Christmas Day in Scotland is not as big a day as at home; most festivities are kept for New Year's Day. But my Christmas here has been happily, though quietly, spent. This part of Glasgow is quite attractive, not greatly different from Canadian cities. Ross must be in England, for a Christmas card has arrived from him, postmarked London.

December 26, 1917   Paid a visit to 178 West Princes St., the home of Gordon Colquhoun's people [9th Bty, killed at Passchendaele], but only his father was at home. I expressed my sympathy as best as I could. At night Agnes, Barbara and Mary went with me to see "Cinderella" at the Theatre Royal.

December 28, 1917   Had a part of my uniform fitted this morning. In the afternoon Barbara and I went out to the Cardonald munitions plant, where we saw eight-inch shells in the process of manufacture. Ross and Doug came out from London unannounced this morning. They are spending the night at the Central Station Hotel.

December 30, 1917   We attended church service in Glasgow Cathedral this morning. The rest of the day was passed very quietly and quickly, and all too soon we had to take leave of our hospitable cousins and proceed to catch our train at Central Station. Being still an 'umble ranker, I had to travel in the special "Naval and Military" train leaving at 10 p.m., fifteen minutes later than the Scottish express with Ross and Doug aboard.

December 31, 1917   Arrived at Euston about 8:15 this morning and followed Ross and Doug to the Howard Hotel. There Ewart joined us a little later and Uncle Arthur (our mother's youngest brother) arrived about noon to complete our happy party. In the afternoon we betook ourselves to a photographer and sat for a group picture. A cable of New Year greetings was dispatched home. Being unable to obtain seats for any of the leading shows, we went to see "Cheep" at the Vaudeville Theatre but found it uninteresting and as cheap as its name. Finished out the day by sitting out the Old Year before a cheerful fire in our room at the hotel.

Thus ended the Old Year, 1917: a year of wonderful experiences both happy and sad, out of which we have all come almost unscathed, protected by the guiding hand of an all-merciful Father. So begins the New Year, 1918: a year filled with the promise of brighter, happier days; a year to which we look forward with confidence and hope and an undaunted faith in the power of a divine Providence to guide our destinies in their proper course whatever may befall. May God grant in His wisdom that this year may see the coming of a victorious peace that shall end for all time the sorrow and the desolation of war.

January 1, 1918 New Year's Day is a Bank Holiday in London; otherwise it is much like any ordinary week day. In the afternoon, following an uneventful morning, we all went to a very excellent concert at Queen's Hall, Oxford Circus. Ewart and I, traveling separately, ran across Percy Fleming and I hope to see him again when I get to Witley. Doug had to return to camp by the 10:00 train from Cannon St., so our happy party has already begun to disperse.

January 2, 1918 The 9:00 train from Waterloo Station this morning bore me quickly away from the scenes of our reunion towards the duties that await me in my new role as a cadet. I reported to the Canadian Artillery Regimental Depot and was duly enrolled in the O.T.C. (Officer Training Corps). My course commenced this afternoon and promises to be a very busy one; so goodbye letter-writing, except for those most important. Don McLaren is here, also Dick Lister and Fred Baragar, whom I knew at the Faculty of Education. We have comfortable quarters and a good cadet mess.

January 3, 1918 A busy day, but beautiful bright frosty weather to keep one feeling fit. Should like to have some mail from home, but don't seem to have time even to write my address to the Glasgow folk, to whom all my mail is presently being sent.

January 5, 1918   Contrary to expectations, we had no test today on the 18-pdr. gun drill which we have been zealously studying during these two and a half days. Probably we shall be given another week of it to ensure a good foundation for the more difficult work to follow. This afternoon was a holiday and I took the opportunity of paying a visit to the 164th Bn lines (Ewart's old battalion). I saw Jessop, Glen, and "Wee" Aiken there, also McCullough (Div. Signals) en route. The weather is rather dull and moderating.

January 6, 1918   Attended service in Witley Church this morning and in the afternoon walked into Godalming to visit Dick and Mrs. Lister. Heavy rainfall part of today, but colder at night. Very beautiful scenery down here in Surrey; I am looking forward to the spring season.

January 7, 1918   Strange how one develops the "Blue Monday" feeling again, with Sunday once more observed as a day of rest (unlike the Sundays in France), but it is only a passing feeling. Today is bright and cold. Met "Cam" Fraser this evening, a former Orangeville boy and a close friend of Ross's boyhood days. Ross is due to enter hospital in London tomorrow for a hernia operation.

January 12, 1918   My first home mail since leaving France arrived Wednesday, dated December 1st. Very cold days have been followed by more moderate weather and plenty of mud. Our class was tested yesterday on gun drill and today we passed out on gun-laying and sight testing; we are listed for Signalling next week. I walked down to Godalming in the afternoon to make a few necessary purchases; it is a busy town with very attractive shops well patronized by Canadian soldiers from the large camps nearby. My companions on the course here are a very fine lot of men and I have been made to feel quite at home by my room-mates, Leathers and Rosebrough and MacDonald and Walford. (not to be confused with Pete Welford of the 67th) Everybody is working hard on the course.

January 14, 1918   A bright sunshiy Sunday was followed by three inches of snow last night. We commenced our Signalling course this morning. Yesterday Uncle Arthur rode over on his bicycle to see me. He has been disappointed in a hoped-for leave to Ireland and now is warned for France— probably in two days' time. I met Allen (of F.O.E., 1914-15).

January 19, 1918   I secured a weekend pass to London and by kindness of Lt. Thompson (Signalling Instructor) was able to catch the 11:43 train this morning. Ran across Stuart Porter on my way to the station but had to postpone any lengthy chat with him. Leaving the train at Clapham Jct., I located No. 3 London General Hospital without much difficulty and found Ross in a cheery little Officers' Ward trying to answer all the letters he has been receiving recently via France. For a patient the gallant captain looked extremely well; he has evidently passed the disagreeable part of the experience and is rather enjoying this enforced rest from soldiering. We had a very enjoyable couple of hours together and my happiness was increased a hundred-fold by the wonderful news of his receipt of a D.S.O.. (Distinguished Service Order). It is a very great honour and richly deserved. I have been for a long time almost certain that some such recognition would come for the services he has rendered, but the sudden realization of my hope leaves me almost speechless—and that's something! Leaving the hospital, I came to Waterloo Station by electric railway, thence to the Howard Hotel where I am spending the night. Passed the evening by myself at the Savoy Theatre where I saw "The Private Secretary," a very clever and amusing play which I had not seen before.

January 20, 1918   Today is the anniversary of my first arrival in France and I have celebrated the day most pleasantly, though with no attempt at appropriateness. Slept until 9:00, breakfasted a half-hour later and spent the remainder of the morning writing letters. The afternoon was again spent at the hospital, where I remained with Ross until time for the 5:37 train for Milford. Was back in camp by 7:30, ready for the beginning of another week's work on Signalling.

January 26, 1918   This week has passed very quickly, with the weather remarkably mild and mostly fair. Yesterday and this morning we had our tests and written exams on Signalling; quite easy for me and for others in the class who had been Signallers. This afternoon I made another trip over to the 164th Bn lines and this time saw quite a number of the Orangeville boys; Alec Saunders, "Wee" Aiken, Finlay

McGillivray, Earl Hewson, Oscar Hayes, George Bull, Franklin Ellis, Harry King, Ernest Statia, a chap named McDougall who attended O.H.S. and Walter Vanwyck (160th Bn). A few days ago I met Gordon Hayes in "Tin Town," our local shopping centre. Yesterday my uniform arrived and is quite satisfactory both in cut and material. It is certainly pleasant to get into good clothes again.

January 27, 1918   Today has been just like a day in May; bright and warm, with never a touch of winter in the air. Just such a day had I been looking for in order to make a visit to the home of the Guys at "Sunnyside" and incidentally, to bring back Uncle Arthur's bicycle left there for my use. By good fortune, I was picked up by an ambulance just outside camp, and soon was around the Devil's Punch Bowl and into Hindhead by 10:30 a.m. An easy walk through Grayshott and along towards Headley soon brought me to my destination and I was so heartily welcomed that I felt immediately well acquainted with these charming people, Mrs. and Miss Guy. The afternoon passed most pleasantly and my return journey in the evening was easily and quickly made on Uncle Arthur's bicycle, down-hill practically all the way.

January 29, 1918   The second day of our Riding course and a first casualty. Cadet Gill, riding a horse that has a tendency to rear, pulled him over on himself and was rather badly hurt.

February 2, 1918   Rain has fallen today, breaking the stretch of beautiful weather with which we have been favoured. The past week has been a strenuous one, under a tough and unsympathetic instructor, but thoroughly enjoyed. This morning we went over the three-foot jumps, with and then without stirrups and reins. My mount "Paddy" is a splendid jumper and so far I have managed to stay with him, even over the water jump. Had my picture taken this afternoon in "Tin Town."

February 8, 1918   Since Monday much rain has fallen daily. We have managed to work in considerable riding each day, but very little jumping or vaulting. Today a number of medals were presented by Maj. Gen. G.B. Hughes. Freddy Donald received his D.C.M. and Cole and Horseman (among others) the M.M. Mine will come up with the next group, probably. Walter Dahl called to see me tonight; he is on draft leave and expects to go to France on Tuesday. Am making a valiant effort to catch up with my letter writing but have a long way to go yet.

February 10, 1918   Alec Hayes came to see me this morning and together we went over to see his brother Gordon and Harold Kilpatrick. Spent this Sunday evening again with Dick and Mrs. Lister in Godalming; a pleasant little taste of home life.

February 13, 1918   The Fifth Division (Inf.) is being broken up and quite a number of the Orangeville boys expect to leave on draft soon to join the 116th Bn in France. The riding course progresses favourably in spite of its constant "ups and downs."

February 16, 1918   Two months today since I left the 9th Bty in France and six weeks of my course have passed into history. Last night I went over to the Garrison Theatre to see the very interesting pantomime "Babes in the Woods," an enjoyable diversion after a strenuous week's work. Met Franklin Jackson this afternoon.

February 17, 1918   Church Parade this morning to No. 4 Y.M.C.A. A beautiful, bright and frosty day; ideal for walking, so I hope to walk down to the Congregational Church in Godalming for evening service.

February 19, 1918   Ewart arrived in camp on a surprise visit at noon today, having been just now granted graduation leave though he qualified for his wings three or four weeks ago. After my afternoon riding class we went down to Godalming and met Ross, who came in from London on an evening train. We spent a very happy time together. Ross looks well and seems quite recovered from his operation. He and Ewart stayed for the night at The King's Arms in Godalming.

February 20, 1918   This morning I conveniently obtained permission to have a bad tooth fixed up by the dentist. This job was satisfactorily completed by 9:30 and I had the rest of the morning with Ross and Ewart, who then left for London by the 11:43 train from Milford. Milder weather has brought rain today.

February 21, 1918   The cadets' quarters were changed today and now I am one of 15 in Hut #A2. Our new home is hardly as comfortable as the old, nor as well adapted for studying, but we retain our beds and have no great cause for complaint. Our Mess remains as before.

February 22, 1918   I had my last ride on Paddy this morning. This afternoon we were breaking in remounts, as on several previous occasions this week, and tomorrow we pass out from the Horsemastership course. There are a number of 9th Bty men in camp now, en route for Canada along with other married men of the First Contingent. I have seen McManus, Tasker, Cinq-Mars and White. Roper, Footitt, Petrie and Beardmore are also going.

February 23, 1918   Wrote the paper on Horsemastership this morning and so have ceased to be a "jockey." Am billed for the Equipment course next week. I saw Sgts. Petrie and Beardmore today; they expect to leave for Canada about next Wednesday. Went to see a rather good presentation of "Under Two Flags" at the Garrison Theatre tonight.

February 28, 1918   Today's "Canada" contains the official announcement (from the *Gazette*) of my M.M. among a host of others including Don McLaren, Dick Lister (Bar to M.M.), Unwin etc. Last week's issue contained a notice of Ross's D.S.O.. Am having a very busy week on Equipment but hope to finish it on Saturday. My paper on Horsemastership brought me 138 marks; 69%. Leathers and Baragar beat me with 78% and 75% respectively. Saw

Bill Adams (9th Bty) today. Weather chiefly and moderately cold but sometimes alternating with rain.

March 2, 1918   I wrote rather a poor paper on Equipment this morning. The Riding results, posted yesterday, gave me "Good"; Leathers and Hay were the only ones who obtained "Very Good." This afternoon the cadets held an At Home in No. 1 Mess; a very pleasant function. Tonight R. Wilson and I went to the Garrison Theatre to see Sir F. Bonson in an abbreviated rendering of "The Merchant of Venice." Rather a disappointment.

March 3, 1918   Having been late on parade Friday noon, I was duly sentenced by today's order to accompany the Guildford picket on its duties for "instructional purposes" tonight. As a result I have spent quite a delightful Sunday evening in town with Windsor and Gillis, my partners in crime. We attended service in the Congregational Church and had a tasty lunch at the Lion Hotel before returning to camp by the 10:00 train. Our duties were nil; the only drawback was that it spoiled all chances of spending the day with Ross at Effingham, as I had hoped to do.

March 4, 1918   Angus's birthday today is duly and affectionately remembered. This morning I commenced Junior Gunnery and expect to put in quite a busy two weeks on the subject. Mackenzie, DePencier and I rented a room in Milford (five minutes' walk from our quarters) and are therefore now able to study in comfort.

March 6, 1918   I received my first letter by aeroplane today. Ewart flew over in his Sopwith "Pup" this morning and dropped a note which was duly delivered to me in the Mess at noon.

Unfortunately, I was attending a lecture at the time and did not see him, though I remember hearing the sound of a plane overhead. A glorious day today, after two or three days of dull weather, has been much enjoyed by all.

March 9, 1918   There was quite a heavy frost last night but today has been wonderfully warm and bright. I have finished just one week of Gunnery, had no examination to write this morning. My mark on Equipment was 78%, to my surprise. A wire from Ross asks me to pay him a visit tomorrow and I rather think I shall do so, weather permitting.

March 10, 1918   Could not find the Adjutant last night, but with an unsigned pass in my pocket I sallied forth this (Sunday) morning, caught the 9:10 train at Milford Station, changed at Guildford, and arrived safely at Effingham Jct. There Ross met me and escorted me to "The Lodge," the beautiful home of Mr. And Mrs. George Pauling, where he has been a guest during his convalescent leave. I was received most kindly by his host and hostess and spent a very enjoyable day. Ross is fortunate indeed to have such a delightful place to while away his holiday. Leaving in the evening by a 5:51 train, I was back in Milford at 7:30. Long looked-for letters from home greeted my return.

March 11, 1918   Fred Baragar has finished the course and left tonight for a 7-days' leave. He is the fourth of the "Old

Guard" to finish, Walford and Rosebrough and Donald having passed out in the order named some time ago. Soon I shall have lost many good friends whose company I joined upon arrival at Witley ten weeks ago.

March 14, 1918 Was delighted to run across Lt. Cliff Henderson this afternoon recently arrived with the 12th Reserve Bn. Hope to see him often during the coming weeks. Have also met Ernie Halbert, formerly of Orangeville. [Cliff, brother of Bill Henderson of the 67th, was later killed in action.]

March 16, 1918 Yesterday we had our tests on Director work and today wrote a paper on Junior Gunnery. I think I did fairly well on both. Next week shall be on a comparatively easy course on Machine Guns. This afternoon MacDonald and I walked to Godalming and from there paddled down the Wye River to Guildford and back: a delightful trip of some four miles each way, and the weather was perfect for such an outing.

March 17, 1918 St. Patrick's Day and mine! To the best of my ability to remember so long a life-span I have now completed twenty-three years on this terrestrial ball—and still going strong! May my twenty-fourth birthday find me no longer engaged in war-like pursuits!

This afternoon I hunted up Cliff Henderson and we spent a pleasant evening together in Godalming.

March 19, 1918 Had another little surprise visit from Ewart last night and this morning. Went to the show with Cliff

Henderson, and this morning we hunted up Bun Aiken who had just reported from hospital to "C" Bty here. Ewart had lunch with me at noon and then returned to London by the 1:53 train from Milford. This afternoon we were treated to an informal little speech (through an interpreter) by a Japanese general who was visiting the camp.

March 22, 1918 Lord French paid a short visit to the camp this afternoon but I saw him only from a distance. The Machine Gun class left for Aldershot on the 6:25 train this evening. We arrived too late to see much of the town and spent the night at the Ash Vale Hotel in North Camp.

March 23, 1918 A most beautiful day for firing on the ranges. We started early and were not finished until 3 p.m. I managed to make a fairly good total but fell down rather badly on "snap shooting." We fired fifty rounds apiece with the Lewis gun, first at 25 and then at 100 yards. The journey back to Witley involved an hour's wait for train connections at Woking; I stopped off for another hour at Guildford, so did not arrive "home" until 7 p.m. "Summer Time" commences at 2 o'clock tomorrow morning.

Fritz's big push in France seems to be making considerable headway, so I guess we'll have a busy summer pushing him back again.

March 26, 1918 Doug and Ewart arrived in camp this afternoon for "a wee bit visit," both looking well and fit. We all went to the show in the evening and I managed to put them up for the night in my quarters here. MacDonald went on leave today, having finished the course last week. I am now on Intermediate Gunnery.

March 27, 1918 Was busy all morning but had an hour or so with Doug and Ewart at noon before they returned to town (London). Doug intends accompanying Ewart to C.F.S. (Central Flying School) for a flight and then expects to go down for a day with Ross at Seaford. I hope to join him on his return to London for the last day of his leave next Sunday. Saw Capt. Dunkley today.

March 30, 1918 Yesterday was Good Friday but work went as usual. This morning I wrote on Intermediate Gunnery, then left on the noon train for a weekend in London. Doug was waiting for me at the National Hotel, Russell Square, and greeted me with the news that he has been warned for France and granted three extra days of leave. We spent a quiet afternoon, had dinner at the Regent Palace Hotel, and then went to see "A Little Bit of Fluff" at the Criterion. On our way there we ran into Bob Richardson (brother of Marjorie) near Piccadilly Circus. The play at the theatre was only moderately entertaining, but we could not procure seats for any better shows.

March 31, 1918 After a good night's sleep in adjoining rooms we woke to the brightness of a delightful Easter Sunday morning. Breakfast finished, we hurried down to St. Paul's Cathedral and attended service in that magnificent old edifice. Walked back at noon down Ludgate Hill into Fleet St. and the Strand, past the Law Courts, up Kingsway and around the British Museum, and so to the hotel for lunch. After lunch the Tube carried us quickly from Russell Square Station to South Kensington, then to the Royal Albert Hall. The usual Sunday afternoon orchestra concert was in progress, probably the finest music to be heard in London, and for two hours we feasted on the wonderful selections rendered in this immense Hall by the orchestra under Landon Ronald, its famous conductor, and by the assisting soloists, Charles Mott (baritone) and May Henderson (violinist). The opening selection by the orchestra, "Four Old Flemish Folk Songs," was conducted by the composer, Arthur de Greef. Probably the most delightful orchestra number was Mendelssohn's "Midsummer Night's Dream," but all the numbers were thoroughly enjoyed.

Standing in front of the Hall is the big (but not too beautiful) Albert Memorial; beyond it stretch the Kensington Gardens, joined on the right to Hyde Park in one long reach of green grass and budding trees. We crossed over to that famous parade ground of High Society, Rotten Row, and then down along the shore of the Serpentine, alive with boating even so early in the season. Walking on to Hyde Park Corner, we passed along Constitution Hill to Buckingham Palace and the Victoria Memorial, down The Mall past St. James Park on one side and St. James Palace (home of Queen Alexandra) on the other, into Whitehall (where the gorgeous Horse Guards stand on guard) and thence into Trafalgar Square. We had tea at the Charing Cross hotel and then returned to Russell Square for dinner in the evening. It was a thrilling day for me, for I had really seen but little of London previously; also it has been a rare treat to be with Doug again before he must return to the Inferno across the Channel. I took the ten o'clock train back to camp, arriving about midnight.

April 1, 1918   This is April Fool's Day, but no one seems to be celebrating it here this year; too many serious matters to think about, I guess. This morning I commenced a week's work on Military Law and Interior Economy: rather an uninteresting subject so far. Stuart Porter is leaving on draft tomorrow and was around to see me tonight. He is looking well but I hate to see him go back to France so soon.

April 6, 1918   Wrote a fair paper on Administration this morning, I think. My mark on Intermediate Gunnery last week was only 73, so I shall have to study a bit harder. Next week it's to be Map Reading.

I ordered a jacket, breeches and a Wolseley Valise (with Kapok sleeping bag) at Hacker in Guildford this afternoon.

April 7, 1918   The weather looked rather forbidding this morning, but after Church Parade I decided to chance the rain and wheeled over to "Sunnyside." Spent a very pleasant few hours with Mrs. and Miss Guy and got back to camp in time for tea. The rain caught me on the return trip, but I had my trench coat and suffered little discomfort.

A letter from Marjorie Richardson had given me a long-distance introduction to an acquaintance of hers recently arrived at Witley, Garrett Williamson by name. I looked him up tonight and found him, as expected, an exceedingly fine fellow, a graduate of the School of Science at Toronto (1910). I hope to see him frequently while we are together here.

April 13, 1918   Wrote a fair paper on Map Reading this morning and then journeyed to Guildford for a fitting of my new jacket. Tonight I went with Bun Aiken and Don McLaren and Harry Waugh to see "The Manxman" by Hall Caine. News has just now reached us here of Bert Wheelock's accidental death on March 19th.

April 14, 1918   Bun and I paid Cliff Henderson a visit this afternoon and found him getting ready for a draft leaving about Tuesday for France. Intended to go to church tonight but the weather has turned too cold and blustery with a promise of rain.

April 20, 1918   Finished off Ammunition this morning and am listed for Manoeuvres next week. Hope the weather clears a bit for that course; it has been very wet for days past. Met Verral Dedrick yesterday.

April 27, 1918   Have had some splendid outings this week on Manoeuvres: fine spring weather, a good horse and a most interesting countryside to explore. Dick Lister and I worked together on the various assignments, with a fair measure of success. On Monday we did a road reconnaissance which took us out through Hambledon and Hanscombe and then up into Godalming. Tuesday we pulled off a brilliant advance against enemy forces in the neighbourhood of

Thursley and Elstead. On Wednesday we sketched most realistic (?) panoramic representations of trench systems out on Hankley Common. Thursday we accompanied a battery on its manoeuvres, acting in such capacities as Section Commander, Captain, Sergeant-Major, etc. Yesterday we fought an heroic rear-guard action out near Hindhead, successfully stemming the enemy's advance and inflicting heavy losses on his mass formations. This morning, however, Capt. Wills (our instructor) presided at a solemn arm-chair postmortem in the Mess at which we were individually reminded of all the sins of omission and commission of which we had been guilty during the week.

I made a fruitless trip to Guildford this afternoon: my clothes were not ready for me. On return to camp I found a wire from Ross and one from Ewart. Delay in receiving these spoiled a weekend reunion, which put me very much out of humour for the rest of the day. Sgt. Bristow is spending the night with me, having come over (with Wilkinson and Kulp) to take the R.A.F. course.

King George invested Ross with the D.S.O. at Buckingham Palace today, to the immense satisfaction of the Clan Macpherson in general and this member of the Clan in particular, namely me.

April 28, 1918   Heavy rain today has disappointed our hopes for a pleasant weekend. However, my correspondence profited a bit thereby. Ewart is at Sunnyside but to wheel over there is out of the question. I can only hope that he might drop off on his way back to town.

April 29, 1918   Commenced two weeks of Senior Gunnery this morning, with only a short course on Gas to go after that. Made 95% on Ammunition; but Capt. Mills gave me a paltry 66 on Manoeuvres, which helps to keep my average from soaring too high! Ewart has gone to Scotland, but I hope to see him this weekend.

May 5, 1918   Last night Ross and Ewart arrived in Godalming and we all went to a show there with Bun Aiken. This (Sunday) morning, after Church Parade, Ross and I went up to see Lt. Dunkley (1st C.O.R.D.). In the afternoon the three Macphersons walked to Guildford and spent an hour paddling on the river in spite of a nasty little drizzle of rain. We attended the evening service in the Methodist Church in Godalming. Ross and Ewart have to return to London by an early train tomorrow, so I bade them goodbye tonight, leaving them to enjoy the comfortable hospitality of the Angel Hotel.

May 6, 1918   I had a rather bad attack of the "Blue Monday" feeling this morning. It's a good thing my course is nearly finished for I'm becoming fed up with studying. Anyway, I can look forward to seven days' leave at the end of it!

May 8, 1918   H.M. King George V honoured us with a flying visit this afternoon accompanied by Gen. Turner, Sir Edward Kemp and other notables. However, few of us saw him except from afar off; for the authorities here, doubtless wishing to impress His Majesty with the patriotic industry of all ranks, kept us closed up in our classrooms right throughout the noon hour and until the king had taken his departure. But some good came of it, for we were given the balance of the day free!

On a sudden inspiration I mounted my gallant bicycle and betook myself, with Cadet Kuhring for company, to Compton and there visited a very fine gallery containing many of the original paintings of G.F. Watts. Nearby is a beautiful little memorial chapel in the centre of a cemetery where the great artist lies buried. We returned "home" via Farnham by the road that runs from Guildford along the crest of the Hog's Back, from which can be seen on either side a wonderful stretch of country. From Farnham the road leads straight through Elstead to Milford. Altogether, we probably covered some 20 or 25 miles. Now I'm beginning to wish that I might have a month or two more to enjoy these beautiful surroundings before returning to France! Cancel entry of May 6th!

May 10, 1918   Was called up today to sign certain papers in connection with transfer of my bank account, so I guess my commission will go through shortly.

This week's "Canada" reports Harry Lewis as missing since April 6th, but Don McLaren has word from home that he is a prisoner of war [unfortunately this proved untrue].

May 15, 1918   On Gas this week and this morning we went through the gas chamber. It is a satisfaction to know that one's respirator is so completely effective even in such a strong concentration of gas, both lachrymatory and chlorine. I thought I had written a poor paper on Senior Gunnery Saturday but the results give me 75%, so I finish up tomorrow for sure. Ross is warned for France again and I am hoping we shall have some leave together.

Harry Firth is back in England, having been returned as "under age"— tells me he may be sent home.

COMMISSIONED LIEUTENANT

May 17, 1918   My course finished yesterday. I spent this morning following my papers through the long process necessary to make me a lieutenant and get me started on a six-day leave. At noon I blossomed forth with two pips on each shoulder, a sling on my Sam Browne belt and no white hat band to keep on adding to my weekly laundry bill. The 1:53 train took me up to the "Big Smoke," where I immediately proceeded to draw my kit allowance of £42 from the pay office. Registered with Herb Davis at the National Hotel and later enjoyed a good laugh at "Yes Uncle" at the Princes Theatre. My leave is to last until Thursday noon and I shall then be on draft for France. No sign of Ross up here but I hope to connect with him tomorrow.

May 18, 1918   Ross arrived this afternoon: too late to go to Upavon today, so we made a little expedition with Barbara Macpherson up the river [Thames] to Richmond and enjoyed a very pleasant evening. I have already done most of my necessary purchasing of kit and am out for a real holiday for the balance of my leave.

May 19, 1918   The 9:15 train from London landed us at Pewsey at noon today, where Ewart met us and escorted us to

C.F.S. (Central Flying School, Upavon). Both Ross and I had a "flip" with Ewart, each of us in turn, this afternoon during which he put us through the "loop," "half roll" and other interesting little stunts. Tennis and the movies whiled away the evening hours.

May 20, 1918   Ewart was busy with his pupils all morning, so Ross and I played tennis. This afternoon one of Ewart's "birds" got lost and landed away over near Bristol. So Ewart went after him, taking Ross as a passenger. I have been out of luck for a "flip" today; spent a quiet evening strolling around the camp.

May 21, 1918   Ross and I were setting out across country this morning to catch the 7:38 train, but Lt. Busk and Lt. Oliver called us back and offered to fly us down to the station. Needless to say, the offer was gratefully accepted and a half-hour later we were up in the air (in two different planes) for a final flight. Our pilots landed us skilfully in a little field by the railway station, and then just as skilfully took to the air again and circled away out of sight. Just before the train arrived, Ewart came over in his "bus" and circled low above us two or three times.

Ross went through to Seaford, so I put in the afternoon with Barbara M. seeing "The Maid of the Mountains" and spent the evening in Regent's Park.

May 22, 1918   I purchased a Lensatic Compass and one or two other articles this morning. In the afternoon Barbara and I went to see "Chu Chin Chow" at His Majesty's Theatre: a most wonderful play which I would have been sorry to miss. Wandered through Hyde Park and Kensington Gardens this evening. A heavy thunderstorm broke over London tonight, putting an end to the nice weather we have had of late. Am staying at the Royal Automobile Club in Pall Mall. Ross wires that he is still awaiting orders; I shall not see him again before returning to camp.

May 23, 1918 Reported back from leave this noon and find I am not on draft for a week or so yet. I might just as well have been given another two or three days in London!

May 24, 1918 Victoria Day is not a general holiday in this country, but the troops were given the day off and a programme of sports was arranged in Guildford.

May 26, 1918 Wheeled over to Sunnyside this afternoon to say goodbye to the people there. It looks now as though I shall be for France about next Saturday. Had photographs taken in Godalming yesterday.

May 27, 1918 Was inoculated this morning and spent the rest of the day very pleasantly with Stan Thompson at the West Surrey Golf Club. On return to camp I ran across Lt. Ferguson (18th Dn.) and had a most interesting chat with him. He went to France almost the same time as I, came back for his commission just two days later than I, and now is to return to France almost on the same day. In his eleven months at the front he has been awarded both the M.M. and Bar.

May 30, 1918   Am ordered to France by Saturday's boat from Folkestone. Hope to spend tomorrow evening in London with Ewart.

May 31, 1918   Met Ewart here in London and accompanied him on a visit to the Countess of Harrowby, Grosvenor Place, who has very kindly arranged for Ewart a few days' holiday in a country home in Leicestershire. We spent a pleasant evening with Barbara M. and are staying together for the night at the National Hotel. Off to France tomorrow. Saw Horace McGuire.

June 1, 1918   Leaving Victoria Station at 7:50 a.m., our little party, with many others returning to France, reached Folkestone two hours later and spent most of the day there. The following are with me from Witley Camp: Lister, Davis, DePencier, Alexander, Dudley, Howland, Hill, Montgomery, Stubbs and Phinney. Our boat sailed about six o'clock and we reached Boulogne, after a smooth and uneventful crossing, some time after 8 p.m. The Officers' Club was crowded, so several of us sought out the Hotel de Paris and spent a comfortable night there. Dinner, bed and breakfast cost us 20 francs ($4.00) apiece.

June 2, 1918   A train leaving at 8:30 this morning took us slowly over the thirty kilometres to Etaples, where we had a good lunch at the excellent Officers' Club near the station and then walked up to the Base Depot. There we found Hay, McInerny, Van Patter, Smith, James and Blizzard still remaining of those who had preceded us in previous drafts.

Blizzard was wounded in the hand by one of the bombs that have fallen in this vicinity in recent enemy raids with disastrous effects on hospitals.

Happening to glance through the *Canadian Gazette* of May 30th this evening, I found out that Ross has been further honoured by being "Mentioned in Despatches" by Sir Douglas Haig "for distinguished and gallant services and devotion to duty." Among others on the list are also Gerald Preston, Maj. Cook (9th Bty) and Lt. Col. MacDonald (O.C. 3rd Bde C.F.A.).

June 3, 1918 A trip by electric tram to Paris-Plage made an interesting diversion this afternoon. This place in normal times is a popular summer resort, but now its streets and its beautiful long beach are well-nigh deserted except for the visiting soldiery. Evidently we are to have an easy week here before proceeding up the line; some of us will have a turn at Orderly Officer but I am well down the list. Smith and the others who arrived here ahead of us are to go forward early tomorrow morning.

June 4, 1918 Spent the morning down at the Gas School and tested my respirator again in the gas chambers. The rest of the day passed very lazily. At tea I was surprised to run across Lt. Ferguson again. He has just come over from Blighty and is attached to our Mess while waiting to go up the line. Went for a walk through the town in the evening.

June 5, 1918   Helped censor letters for an hour this morning. Montgomery is Orderly Officer today and Alexander is next for duty.

June 7, 1918   Among letters censored this morning was one from someone in camp here to Harold Marshall, R.C.H.A. (Royal Canadian Horse Artillery). I sent along my good wishes. Dick Lister went up to the C.C.R.C. [Canadian Corps Reserve Camp] early this morning in charge of a small draft of men. The rest of us should follow along about the beginning of the week.

June 9, 1918   Last night another draft arrived from the O.T.C. at Witley. That should hasten our marching orders. Campbell, Adams, McLean, Knapman and Borbridge are among the newcomers.

Attended a Church Parade this morning and in the afternoon went over to see A.B. MacDonald, who is on an M.G. (Machine Gun) course at Le Touquet. While there I met Lt. Robertson of the 16th Bn and gave him a message for Doug.

RETURN TO THE FRONT: FRANCE

June 11, 1918   Orders came yesterday for all the C.F.A. officers to proceed up the line. So this morning, after an early breakfast, some eighteen of us said goodbye to Etaples and boarded a train bound for Calonne Ricourt. Long stops at intermediate points (notably at St. Pol) delayed us and it was early afternoon before we arrived at our destination and reported to the C.C.R.C.. There we were informed that we shall probably be going farther on our way "to the war" tomorrow; in the meantime we are to spend the night at various billets in the town to which we have been directed. Davis and I are sharing a room in a tidy little house near one of the big mines (Fosse 6). Alexander and Knapman are in an adjoining room.

This evening Alex and I walked over to Marles-les-Mines and had a pleasant little visit with some friendly French people with whom he had become acquainted last fall.

After being taken for Angus by an officer (Lt. Bourke) at the base a few days ago, it was rather amusing today to be greeted as "Doug" by a chap (MacDougall, 52nd Bn) who knew Doug and Angus in Moose Jaw, who had just arrived from Aubin St. Vaast. It was only after a rather confusing attempt at conversation that he began to be convinced that he had made a mistake in my identity. Thank goodness, these brothers of mine have not too bad a reputation or I would be having an uncomfortable time of it out here!

Tomorrow should decide what Division I am to go to.

June 12, 1918   Our party has been badly split up today. Alexander, among others, has gone to the 3rd D.A.C.; Davis and others have gone to the 5th; and I, with Howland and Campbell, am on my way to the 2nd. A train at 12:30 brought us back to St. Pol. After a wait of several hours we entrained again for Aubigny, where we are spending the night at the Officers' Club.

June 13, 1918   The narrow gauge railway brought us here to

Monchiet this afternoon and we are now temporarily attached to No. 3 Section of the 2nd D.A.C. The length of our stay and our subsequent destination are as yet unknown. Dick Lister is here, also Lt. Wallace whom I knew at Witley. A game of baseball this evening gave us some much needed exercise.

June 14, 1918   With no assigned duties for the day, I went off on a tour with three companions on a motor lorry which took us to Avesnes-le-Compte, Frevent, Doullens and back. The lorry was sent for canteen supplies and we had lengthy stopovers at the last two places. The country looks attractive but the roads are very dusty except where tarred.

Hay and Clarke arrived today, having been transferred from the 5th and 3rd D.A.C. respectively.

June 15, 1918   After attending to a few very minor duties this morning, several of us walked over to witness a ball game between the 18th and 26th Bns which the 26th won by a wide margin. We had a game of our own in the evening.

June 16, 1918   The merry month of June has passed into its second half and I am still very much a gentleman of leisure. Today, however, I was Orderly Officer for No. 3 Section, to which Lister and I are both attached, and so had a few extra duties to attend to. Have suddenly developed a cold and fever. Should be O.K. in the morning.

June 18, 1918   Had a rotten time with my cold yesterday, but a few aspirin tablets seem to have taken away the fever and now I'm all right except for a bad throat. Played shortstop for the D.A.C. against the 2nd Div team this afternoon. Sad to say, we went down to defeat!

June 21, 1918 Mother's birthday and Doug's duly remembered. However, being Orderly Officer, I couldn't declare a holiday for myself in honour of the occasion. A letter from Doug indicates that he is only 15 or 20 kilometres from here and I am going to try to get over to see him before I am moved again.

June 23, 1918 I met Lt. Ferguson again today at the 2nd Div. sports held in Basseux. He is with his old battalion now, the 18th.

June 24, 1918 Business being far from brisk, I rode out on Capt. Jackson's charger in search of Doug. Found him at Ecoivres and spent a most happy few hours with him there. Came back through a heavy downpour of rain but that did not spoil my enjoyment of the ride.

Encouraging news comes from the Italian front these days, but it's "all quiet on the Western front." How much longer will it be, I wonder, before my services are required up the line? Am becoming "fed up" with idleness.

June 27, 1918 My first Canadian mail re-addressed from Witley came in three days ago. Today I have received 12 Canadian letters via Glasgow. In a letter that came yesterday from Ross I learn to my delight that the Univ. of Saskatchewan has granted him his B.A. in absentia.

June 28, 1918 After three months in action on this front the entire (2nd) Div. is pulling out on rest. Our D.A.C. does not move until Sunday, but today a lorry load of material from No.1 and 3 Sections was sent to Etrée-Wamin and I came along with it to look over the ground on which we are to encamp and to take over the standings and billets allotted to us. I have found that the 3rd D.A.C. is here en route from Monchiet, so I am enjoying the hospitality of No.2 Section by invitation of T.W. McLean and O'Grady.

Met Alex. Fleming, Hugh Ketchum and Holdsworth: all old 67th men.

June 29, 1918   Spent a busy day today without accomplishing very much. The horse lines allotted for our use are fairly good, but the billets are not very choice and I have been trying to improve a bit on the selection. The village itself is rather pretty and nicely situated; with fine weather we should have a pleasant sojourn. I had dinner this evening at No.3 Section's Mess with Capt. Kruger and Lt. Wilson. The 3rd D.A.C. will pull away from here tomorrow and will pass our column on the way.

June 30, 1918   The column came in about mid-afternoon and already things are fairly well settled down; but a lot of work remains for tomorrow. I am in a billet with Lister and Campbell, well fixed for a good night's sleep. Two days of tramping about the streets of this wee place have made me footsore and weary.

July 1, 1918   Too busy as Orderly Officer to celebrate Dominion

Day with much enthusiasm but, in spite of work to be done, a half-holiday was granted the men this afternoon. Some of them were permitted to go to Tineques by motor lorry to witness the Corps Sports being held there.

July 2, 1918   The 17th Bty moved into the village yesterday afternoon and with it I find several old friends: Jake Irwin, Bill Henderson and F.B. Smith. First time I have seen Lt. Irwin since Shorncliffe days. Lt. A.R. Wilson is also an officer in this unit but is away on a short course somewhere.

July 4, 1918   I have been detailed to conduct a series of lectures on Map Reading for a group of N.C.O.s and men, commencing at the beginning of next week. This afternoon Lister and I rode into Avesnes-le-Compt to make a few purchases. I managed to buy a much needed pair of light-weight sox for 6½ francs.

A letter from Maj. Cook has reached me today, evidently after a long chase. It dates back to June 10th and states that he has made an application for me to be posted back to the 9th Bty. I have been doubtful of the advisability of an officer returning to a unit in which he had served in the ranks, but the Major does not seem to agree with that theory. It is gratifying that he is willing to have me back again.

July 7, 1918   Attended a communion service at 9 o'clock this morning and Church Parade at 9:45. After the church service Gen. Panay presented medal ribbons to Sgt. Johnston and several other N.C.O.s and men of the D.A.C. Went for a long walk with Lister in the afternoon. By a letter from Doug I learned that I missed seeing him and Ross and Uncle Arthur by not being able to attend the Corps Sports on Dominion Day.

July 8, 1918   My duties as Orderly Officer, in addition to the special course in Map Reading, have given me quite a busy day. My class consisted of five men from each of the three Sections of Column (D.A.C.) and I am to have an hour daily with them all this week.

Concerning officer personnel of the 2nd D.A.C.: Col. Harrison, D.S.O., is O.C. of the Column and Capt. L. F. Jackson is O.C. the 3rd Section, to which I am attached. The subalterns belonging to this Section are Lts. Wallace, Wurtele and Clarke. Campbell, Lister and Kitchen, like myself, are only temporarily attached. Capt. Gamblin and Capt. Routier are in command of No.1 and No.2 Sections, respectively.

July 9, 1918   Had a short visit from Lt. Baragar today while he was over to see his old friends in the 17th Bty. It was a great pleasure to see him again and he gave me news of several mutual acquaintances.

Rain has come at last to break a long spell of hot summer weather: an agreeable change if it does not last too long.

July 13, 1918   Wound up the Map Reading course today with a full morning's work on the hillside above the village. I think most of the class derived some benefit from my instruction; I quite enjoyed the week's work myself.

Had a long chat this evening with Errol Shaver of No.2

Section, formerly 67th Bty. The weather continues rather unsettled and there is now considerable mud to contend with instead of dust. But on the whole we are having an enjoyable rest from active soldiering.

July 14, 1918   Capt. Ormond, Chaplain of the 5th Bde C.F.A., conducted the church service this morning. He was formerly our Chaplain in the Toronto Bde at Petawawa and I had quite a pleasant chat with him after the service. This afternoon sudden orders arrived for us to clear out of our happy home here by tomorrow morning. Later details named Montenesecourt as our destination. Once again the billeting job is "to me" and I have to leave at 6 a.m. Heavy rain tonight.

July 15, 1918   A leisurely ride brought me to Montenescourt about 9:30 this morning. Howland and Ness came along to take over for No.1 and No.2 Sections, respectively. The 56th British Division, whom we are relieving, does not pull out until the end of the week but we have managed to squeeze in beside them fairly comfortably for the intervening days. The Column pulled in at 1 o'clock and everybody was fairly well settled by early evening. Campbell and I are in a tent which, fortunately, is giving us good protection from a wild thunderstorm that has come upon us.

July 17, 1918   Had a trip to Savy and Aubigny today for a mess-cart load of explosives. In passing through Hermanville, I saw "Wee" Aiken and stopped to chat with him for a minute or two.

July 18, 1918   An excursion to Warlus today in search of further items to be added to No. 3 Section's mobilization stores proved in vain, and I narrowly missed a heavy downpour of rain coming back. This afternoon Jack Stirre came over form the 1st D.A.C. and through him I have found still another 67th Bty man in this Column: Haldenby of No.1 Section.

We are to move again, this time to Savy or maybe farther. We seem to have a roving commission lately.

July 19, 1918   Rode out from camp about 8 o'clock this morning and arrived at our new home (Vendelicourt) in time to have things well arranged for No.3 Section before the Column pulled in. We are in G.H.Q. Reserve and therefore do not know when we may be called on to move to any part of the line. No.3 Section has an exceptionally good Mess here, with billets attached; but Clarke and I are living, by preference, in a tent.

July 20, 1918   Dick Lister and I rode over to Tineques this morning to try out a couple of new saddle horses we are taking for temporary use. Both mounts are quite good and we had a very enjoyable ride. Heavy rain this afternoon, with cooler weather following.

News from the Franco-American front is very encouraging lately. Our own front is lively and there is considerable enemy bombing at night, even back here. Today's paper reports Errol Sydie missing; hope for better news later.

July 21, 1918   Am Orderly Officer today; duties light. Kitchen and Lister have been posted to the 5th and 6th Bdes., respectively, and are to leave us in the morning. When will my turn come, I wonder!

July 22, 1918 At last I am back with a fighting unit again. Orders came today for Campbell and me to report to the 5th Bde C.F.A. Campbell has gone to the 20th Bty and I am with the 23rd—a 4.5 Howitzer Battery, like the 9th. The 5th Bde is under orders to move tomorrow back to Berlencourt near Etree-Wamin; so my stay in this wee village of Berles is to be very short. I am sleeping tonight in one of the luxurious bedrooms of the chateau here, the windows of which overlook a beautiful stretch of green grass and lovely shade trees. It is a pity to have to move quite so soon.

Division HQ officers defeated the Brigade officers in a good game of baseball this evening. Gen. Pannay plays well on first base and his work with good pitching by Staff Captain Duncan, won the game.

July 23, 1918 Our move has been postponed—and fortunately so, for there has been very heavy rain during most of the day. The O.C., Maj. Paterson, has given me the Right Section to look after. R.B. Leigh is also with the 23rd, so I am not entirely among strangers here. Capt. Tingley and Lt. Waterous (from Brantford) are the only other officers with the battery just now (besides the Major), but Lts. Gillespie, Bick and Minnes are due to return shortly from leave.

July 24, 1918 We were blessed with good weather for the move to Berlencourt today and are now comfortably settled in our new home. I have been Orderly Officer and so rather busy from 5 o'clock Reveille to 10 p.m.

July 27, 1918   Yesterday I was Bde Orderly Officer; today I am similarly employed for our own battery. There has been so much rain since we pulled in here that our horse lines became almost submerged in water. So early this afternoon they were moved to a somewhat better location. I have been splashing back and forth between the old and the new standings until my feet are soaking wet and I am mud from head to foot.

Howard Knight, who is with the T.M.s (Trench Mortars) came over to find his cousin in the Battery here and I had a short chat with him.

Lt. Gillespie has returned from attending a Camouflage course, so my duties will not be quite so heavy as during the past few days.

July 28, 1918   This morning's church service was most enjoyable. It was held in a big Y.M.C.A. tent, and both the singing and Capt. Ormond's address were very inspiring. A piano and a violin to lead in the hymns made a wonderful improvement on the usual outdoor services.

July 29, 1918   Had a ride back to Aubigny today for Mess supplies. In passing through Savy, I ran across Lloyd Patterson and Percy Leighton. Arrived "home" again about 4:30 p.m. Lt. Minnes has returned from leave, so I am relieved of responsibility for the Right Section. Late orders tonight give warning of another move.

July 31, 1918   Leaving Berlencourt after 10 o'clock last night, the

Brigade completed the first stage of a sudden move southwards about 5 a.m. this morning, after covering about 25 kilometres (15 miles). Our stopping place is the village of Orville, six kilometres out of Doullens. After about four hours' sleep I rode into Doullens with Maj. Patterson and others to make a few purchases. Last night the weather was exceptionally fine and cool for travelling and promises to remain fine for our next 20 miles tonight.

Saw Roy Gall in Doullens.

August 1, 1918　　Now we are in Argoeuvers, some four miles northwest of Amiens which can be easily seen in the distance. The Somme river flows through a marshy valley to the south of the village. We are comfortably settled, for a day and night at least. It seems probable that we shall be going into action on this front. Today and yesterday have been extremely hot.

August 3, 1918　　Our sojourn this time has been of three days' duration, during which both men and horses have rested up a bit. Tonight we continue our journey and once again the weather is favouring the move.

August 4, 1918　　Travelling eastwards through Amiens, early morning found us in the wooded grounds of a chateau beyond the village of Longueau. These are evidently to be our Wagon Lines and our gun positions will be somewhere ahead. Great things are pending in the next few days!

Amiens is apparently a very fine city, though now well-high deserted by its civilian population. I am looking forward to seeing it in daytime. German shells have done considerable damage to some sections but most of its buildings seem to be unharmed. The façade of the cathedral is heavily sand-bagged. I sincerely hope the Hun will soon be too far away to do further damage to this city and many others.

August 6, 1918   Spent a busy day with Capt. Tingley reconnoitring forward areas and now am at our present gun positions assisting in preparations for the strenuous work ahead. Our guns, which were brought up here just tonight, are not firing at all; just laid out on S.O.S. lines for a possible emergency. Much rain and mud today, but there must be better weather ahead.

August 7, 1918   A day of rest and quiet preparation for the morrow. Everything augurs well for the success of our attack on the unsuspecting Hun.

WOUNDED AT THE BATTLE OF AMIENS

August 11, 1918   From the relatively peaceful surroundings of a bed in No.2 Red Cross Hospital in Rouen my narrative can now be continued. Very early on Thursday morning (August 8th) our whole Brigade was drawn up on an open field near Cachy, awaiting the dawn. The roar of the bombardment burst out at 4:20 and immediately one Section of each Battery moved forward towards No Man's Land. Lt. Gillespie and his Centre Section were given this leading role for the 23rd Bty.

Thirty-five minutes later I started forward in command of

the Right Section, preceded by two sections of the 17th Bty and followed by Lt. Waterous and his Left Section. The march to our old front line was uneventful, but there we met the Hun's counter-barrage and our difficulties began. The 17th Bty suffered some casualties and pulled off the trail into a neighbouring field to reorganize. So far as I could see ahead through the mist and smoke, however, no great obstacles had been encountered; and, taking with me a man from "A" Subsection, I went forward to reconnoitre the road, leaving my Section back in the unshelled area behind. Finding the track apparently O.K., I started back to bring on the guns.

But a shell got me rather badly, unfortunately killing the poor chap with me (Gnr. Gallagher). For some time I lay helpless and only partly conscious. Then "Wat." came up to investigate my prolonged absence and, going back immediately to the guns, sent up two men to look after me. I was carried to the shelter of a muddy trench, where my various wounds were roughly dressed; and there I remained for a long time waiting for stretcher-bearers. Although I had lost a lot of blood, I managed to retain partial consciousness, even during the subsequent rough journey back to the dressing station at Cachy. From there an ambulance carried me back to the 1st Canadian Field Ambulance and, later, to No.5 Casualty Clearing Station at some railhead still unknown to me. I was finally put aboard a Red Cross train which landed me in Rouen Friday morning.

My face was first X-rayed and then I went under an anaesthetic while Fritzie's steel fragments were removed from my person. I appear to have a dozen or so punctures altogether, but only three or four are severe. A deep gash across the left upper leg just missed the knee. Another deep one in the left side and back fractured a rib and very narrowly missed the kidney and spine. A note-book in my left tunic pocket probably saved me from a smashed hip: a fragment passed right through it and lodged harmlessly about half-an-inch deep in my anatomy. Two pieces struck my face. One entered the left cheek, took out a tooth as it passed through my mouth, and lodged just under the right cheek bone. The other struck higher up and is still buried somewhere under the left eye.

Altogether I appear to have been very fortunate, and it is only by Divine Providence that I am still alive. How long I shall be out of action is hard to judge yet: probably three or four months. I shall be sent on to Blighty from here just as soon as I am able for the journey.

Here everything is bright and cheery and all the nurses are very efficient and helpful. But I hate to be so helpless and the dressing of my wounds sure is agony. Sleep so far is impossible, but matters will improve in that respect. I am most anxious for news of Ross and Doug. I have wired home and also to Ewart.

There seems to be frequent bombings of nearby areas by Fritz.

August 13, 1918   Much relieved to learn through a sergeant in Canadian Records here that Ross and Doug are both safe. A casualty list today shows Lt. Ferguson (18th Bn) as wounded on the 8th; so his war experiences and mine are still coinciding remarkably closely. It will probably be a week or more before I shall be moved to England. The holes in my anatomy are rather large and my temperature keeps too high for an early change. The effects of my face wounds are rather annoying.

August 22, 1918 The days and nights have been long and tiresome in the extreme; and yet the time has passed quickly as I look back over the thirteen days since my arrival here. Now I am resting quite easily and my wounds are healing well. Just now I have been told that I am for England by the next convoy, probably tomorrow, and the prospect is decidedly pleasant. Some fellow Canadians have come into this ward since I arrived, and some Australians, but most of the patients are Imperial officers. I am more than ever impressed with the efficiency of the hospital. All the nurses except the sisters in charge are only V.A.D.s; yet all are most skilful in their work and a very pleasant atmosphere of good cheer pervades the place.

August 23, 1918 Nineteen months ago I stopped overnight in Rouen en route from Le Havre to the front and in the morning re-entrained on a siding immediately alongside the River Seine. This morning, after a painful ride over the cobblestone streets of the city, I was placed aboard a Red Cross train on the same siding and carried swiftly back along the railway line to Le Havre. Reaching there in the early afternoon, I was immediately transferred to the hospital ship *Essequibo*. But it was not until 10 o'clock or later that we pulled out of the harbour bound for Southampton.

In the bed beside me is an Australian officer, Warnock by name, who was a fellow guest of Ewart's during his visit to Leicestershire just after my return to France. Have had quite an interesting chat with him.

August 24, 1918   The night passed uneventfully and fairly comfortably. The *Essequibo* is said to be the steadiest ship on the run and the Channel was on its good behaviour, so no one had any excuse for seasickness. We docked at Southampton about ten o'clock this morning and I was carried directly to a Red Cross train bound for London. A three-hour run brought us to Paddington Station and from there an ambulance carried me quickly to the Prince of Wales Hospital for Officers in Marylebone, NW1. So here I am again in the Big Smoke, established in state in one of the luxurious guest rooms of this (formerly) Great Central Hotel. One other officer only (Lt. Gill) shares the room at present; there are two empty beds. The nursing sisters and attendants are all very helpful. I have wired Ewart and hope he may be able to pay me a visit soon.

August 27, 1918   Through the kindness of my doctor two other Canadian patients have visited me several times and helped me pass the long hours of idleness. One is Lt. C.C. Martin, 6th Bty C.F.A., who knows Gerald Preston and Stuart Porter very well; the other is Lt. F.G. Rounthwaite, 12th Bty, C.G.A. Both are walking about, having nearly recovered from their wounds. As I remarked before, everyone here is very willing and helpful. But there is an obvious lack of system and organization about the place that becomes almost laughable. No one seems to have a definite idea of what he or she is supposed to be doing or of what anyone else is doing. There is a continuous procession entering the room, each one doing some little thing that has probably already been done and all forgetting certain things that ought to be done. In the three days since my arrival I have seen at least twenty different members of the staff. But it is most ungrateful to be critical of those who are my benefactors during these days of helplessness. My wounds are carefully dressed each day and the doctor, an American temporarily in charge on this floor, is admirably efficient. Two other officers (Lts. Scott and Roberts) have been brought in to keep Gill and me company; none of us is in very serious shape. Yesterday a letter arrived from Ewart and I am expecting a visit from him early next week.

August 31, 1918   The arrival of many letters, accumulated for me in Glasgow and France, has helped greatly to pass the long hours of the past three days. My mail from home is well up to date again, including letters written on the 11th after receipt of my cable from Rouen. It is good to know that Angus has managed to get home for a visit. This afternoon Barbara Macpherson came in to see me and her visit added much cheer to the day. Monday will likely bring Ewart.

September 1, 1918   Cadets Mackenzie and Creech, two good friends from Witley, came to see me today and gave me much welcome news of mutual acquaintances. Barbara also called again, and the afternoon passed very pleasantly. In the evening I had my first little toddle around the room: an agreeable change from lying in bed, but the torn muscles in my back and leg are evidently not ready to carry me very far yet awhile. The side of my face is still more or less dead and the eye and jaws have not improved any yet. I guess time is the cure for this particular trouble. Nice, bright, cool weather for September 1st.

September 2, 1918 Had a happy visit with Ewart this afternoon and hope to see him daily during most of this week.

September 4, 1918 Ewart continues to run in for a chat at frequent intervals daily. With his help I have hunted up a tailor to come here to the hospital to measure me for some necessary clothing. Am not able for a long walk yet, but shall be getting about quite freely by the time my new outfit is ready. The weather is fine and bright.

NEWS OF ROSS MACPHERSON'S DEATH

September 26, 1918 As one in a daze, devoid of all feeling in mind, body and soul, I look back over the dark days and nights that have passed since the news of Ross's death on August 26th reached Ewart and me three weeks ago. I seem to be living in an entirely different world, a dreary place where nothing matters anymore and the weeks and months and years stretch out ahead in hopeless emptiness and unspeakable loneliness. But such an attitude is unworthy of the loved one whom God in his wisdom has taken from us after a career unsurpassed in its brilliant and devoted service to a great cause. May God grant us the strength and courage to carry on as Ross would have us do, in spite of the sorrow that has come so heavily upon us all. It is comforting and inspiring to know, both by cablegrams and by letters just now to hand, that our home folk and Marjorie are bearing up so wonderfully under the sudden blow. But my heart aches for their suffering and their loneliness, which I can do nothing to ease.

Ewart was with me until Saturday, the 7th, when he had to return to his duties at C.F.S. His presence with me meant much to both of us in the first few days of our common sorrow. But after his departure the enforced idleness and confinement in the hospital was well-nigh unbearable. The arrival of my kit from France on the 10th gave me clothes to wear and two days later I made my first venture outside: a tremendous relief after five weeks' imprisonment. Almost daily since then I have been out to various parts of the city, and now I am hoping to be considered fit for a trip down to see Ewart this coming weekend.

September 30, 1918   A noon train from Paddington on Saturday landed me at Pewsey about three o'clock and I spent until today noon very pleasantly though quietly with Ewart. The "youngster" has at last succeeded in his efforts to obtain permission to give up his instructor's work, and a few weeks at the most will see him in France. It will be hard to see him go!

October 2, 1918   Since nearly a week ago I have been located on the fifth floor of the hospital in Room 560 with Lts. Fairweather (C.G.A.), Bond (3rd London Regt.) and Fraser (Black Watch). I have been able to discard the bandage on my leg and the back wound, too, is well-nigh healed; so it seems likely that another week or so will witness my removal to some other hospital. Nothing has been done for my jaw or eye, although a dozen or more X-Ray plates have been taken.

October 4, 1918   Doug arrived unexpectedly in town last night on leave from France, to my surprise and delight, and I have been with him all day today. I have applied for another weekend leave so that I may spend tomorrow and Sunday and Monday with him.

October 6, 1918   I have been free from hospital since yesterday morning. Stayed overnight with Doug at the Hotel Rembrandt (out in Kensington) and this morning we journeyed down to Headley for a "wee bit visit" with the Guys. The weather is fine and the country looks very beautiful in the bright fall sunshine.

October 7, 1918   Back to London by an early train today. Doug left at noon for Upavon; Ewart may return with him tomorrow or Wednesday.

October 8, 1918   Late last night my transfer orders arrived and today noon a train from St. Pancras Station bore me swiftly north into the Midlands. Now I am comfortably established in my new home, the Canadian Convalescent Hospital at Matlock Bath, Derbyshire.

October 10, 1918   Lts. Bick and Burnett and Leigh are here with me: all from the 23rd Bty. Burnett is the officer whose place I took in the battery last July. It is a good place, this; but the doctors here may lack the necessary equipment for treating my stubborn old jaw.

October 13, 1918   Bick and I attended morning service at the Wesleyan Methodist Church in Matlock today. This afternoon we went for a long tramp over the summit of the High Tor, one of the chain of hills that almost completely encircles this quaint old village of Matlock Bath. Am gaining strength rapidly now and shall soon be feeling quite fit. Capt. Alec Bowles arrived here a day or two ago: the same old Alec of high school days, but with an arm temporarily in a sling and an M.C. ribbon on his tunic.

The war news is very encouraging these days, with much talk of an early peace—especially since Bulgaria retired from the fight on September 30th. But Germany will have to be soundly whipped before we shall obtain a peace worth having.

October 15, 1918   I had planned to join a party going from here to Chatsworth House, the home of the Duke of Devonshire, Canada's Governor General. But I had to remain in the hospital for a consultation with Lt.Col. Turner, a consulting specialist and a brother of Gen. Turner, V.C. This doctor recommends careful examination of my jaw under an anaesthetic and I shall probably have to go to Buxton for that.

October 17, 1918   Arrived in Buxton, Derbyshire, this afternoon along with Alec Bowles and four other officers requiring special treatment. New address: Granville Canadian

Special Hospital, formerly the Palace Hotel.

Doug's leave expired this morning, so he is doubtless now on his way back to France. I am hoping the Canadian Corps will be out of the active fighting for some time, after a recent series of heavy and costly engagements. The war news continues to be encouraging, but it all seems to matter so little now that Ross is no longer with us to witness the final success of the cause for which he fought so long and so brilliantly.

October 19, 1918   Was X-Rayed again today and also received the first instalment of the massage treatment prescribed for my face. At least two other old Orangeville boys are at present in Buxton: Capt. Fred Mathews of the C.A.M.C. and Fred Patterson, who was with the 75th Bn. The latter has lost his left leg but is looking fairly well. One of the three officers with whom I am quartered in Room 45 is Lt. McGeary of the 38th Bn, who was a ranker in Ross's company of the P.P.s. It is a pleasure to hear him speak so highly of Ross's bravery and leadership under all conditions.

October 21, 1918   More X-Rays and no verdict yet! Daily massage treatment continues however, and this should soon <u>ease</u> matters a little.

October 23, 1918   Buxton is a great place for long, interesting walks and already McGeary and I have explored the countryside in several directions. The town itself is beautifully laid out, with well-kept streets and parks, good shops of all kinds, and handsome residences. The population is given as some

10,000 but from the great number of hotels and its reputation as a popular inland health resort it is evident that its peace-time summer population would be very much above this figure. This afternoon I spent at Poole's Cavern, a most interesting place with marvellous rock formations and historic associations.

October 25, 1918   Col. Turner held his weekly examination of surgical patients today and seemed quite satisfied with my progress. Evidently he no longer considers an operation necessary and counts on massage treatment to bring my jaw back to normal. The eye, also, seems somewhat improved.

A wire from Ewart this evening states that he is in London until Monday, so I am trying to wangle a pass for the weekend.

October 26, 1918   A 12:45 train from Buxton (via Nottingham) landed me in London at 6:30. Ewart met me at St. Pancras Station and after dinner at the R.A.C. (Royal Automobile Club) we went to the Haymarket Theatre to see "The Freedom of the Seas," rather a good show. We are staying at the Regent Palace Hotel for these two nights.

October 28, 1918   Our few hours together passed by all too quickly but were greatly enjoyed by both of us. Ewart had to leave by a noon train from Liverpool Station for No.3 School of Fighting at Bircham Newton, Norfolk, where he is to receive a few days' final instruction before proceeding to France. But first he saw me off by the 9:35 from St. Pancras, which returned me to Buxton at 2:15 p.m. (165 miles). Garfield

Gordon, Lt. C.G.A., is here for just a few days en route to Canada on a six months' sick leave. I am sending home with him Doug's German revolver and dagger and a few things of Ross's, as well as my "precious" M.M.

Tonight's mail has brought from Doug the splendid news that he has been awarded the Military Cross. Am very much delighted that his good services have at last been given due recognition.

October 31, 1918   Ewart announces by wire this evening his return to London and his departure for France on Saturday. He leaves a brilliant record behind him at C.F.S. and will undoubtedly give a good account of himself "over there." Each day's newspapers tell of startling developments in the war situation and one becomes almost bewildered by the rapidity of events on all fronts. This evening we learn that Turkey has capitulated, following on the defection of Bulgaria just a month ago and the total rout of her armies in Mesopotamia and Palestine. The Italians are making rapid progress against the Austrian forces and the final surrender of the Dual Monarchy is probably only a matter of hours. Fritz will doubtless fight on for yet awhile but the end seems well in sight.

November 1, 1918   By the exercise of his magic power of painless extraction the dentist today skilfully relieved me of the jagged roots of the incisor I lost on a certain day back in August. Next week I may persuade him to put in a new one for me. The jaw is still coming along nicely, but it looks like a long process yet. My back wound evidently did not appreciate the removal of bandages some three weeks ago; once again it demands a dressing every second day, and this after nearly three months in hospital.

November 4, 1918   Austria is out of the fight, from today. Germany is alone now.

November 5, 1918   Visited Chatsworth House this afternoon with McGeary, travelling by train to Bakewell and thence by "horse power." An exceptionally fine day added much to our enjoyment of the trip.

November 8, 1918   Some snow fell today, making this first week of November quite like the late autumn in Canada. Excellent weather for long walks and McGeary and I have taken full advantage of it. The patients at the Palace held a tea and dance this afternoon at which I met a number of the nursing sisters from various hospitals in Buxton. Among them were two (Miss Bindon and Miss Shand) who knew Dr. Carson at Orpington.

The Huns were handed the Allied armistice terms by Marshal Foch today and given seventy-two hours in which to accept or reject them. It seems quite possible that the end of this ugly war business is really now at hand.

ARMISTICE

November 11, 1918   The war came to an end at 11 o'clock this morning, for the Germans have signed such a formidable array of armistice terms as to preclude beyond a doubt any chance of reopening hostilities. Boisterous celebrations are in progress in Buxton and doubtless throughout all the Allied countries. If only Ross had lived to see this day!

November 13, 1918   Letters from Doug and Ewart received today have given me reasonable assurance of their safety right to the finish and I have cabled home an "All well." McGeary departed for Matlock Bath this morning. Bright, frosty weather.

November 18, 1918   A note from Ewart gives his address now as No. 201 Squadron, France, where he reported from the Pool on the 13th. Have cabled this home so that his Christmas mail may be sent direct.

November 21, 1918   Five weeks in Buxton and the end is not yet! My jaw is steadily improving under the careful and efficient treatment (a mixture of force and persuasion) administered by Miss Binning in the massage department. I have gained almost an inch of clearance and another week or two should restore nearly normal movement. Hope soon to have something done to my crooked old eye.

The days pass very quietly; long walks, billiards, letter-writing and other such pastimes help to fill in the idle hours. Leave has reopened, so I hope soon to pay a visit to Rochdale, beyond Manchester, to see Duncan Fitzpatrick who is in hospital there.

November 25, 1918   Arrived in Rochdale this afternoon and located Duncan without much difficulty. He is looking fairly well and getting about now quite easily; so he was able to come in to dinner with me and later to a show at the

Theatre Royal. The Birch Hill Hospital is out in Dearnley, a suburb of Rochdale, but with good tram service between the two places. Neither place is at all prepossessing in appearance, being evidently given over to industrial activities —chiefly cotton and woolen mills.

November 26, 1918   Duncan came in to the Wellington Hotel, where I spent the night, about 10 o'clock and together we "did the town" including a rather good municipal Art Gallery. An early afternoon train brought me back to Manchester, where I had been hoping to spend a few hours before returning "home" to Buxton. But a miserable rain and mist made sight-seeing far from enjoyable and my first-hand knowledge of the city is still limited to the vicinity of Victoria and London Road Stations and their connecting streets, all unattractive and muddy. Departing from the last-named station at 4 p.m., I arrived in Buxton in time for dinner.

November 29, 1918 A very pleasant sojourn in Buxton came to an end this morning though I may return for further treatment presently. Leaving at 9:40, the Midland Express landed me in London shortly after 2 p.m. A further two-hour trip on the S.E. & C. from Charing Cross brought me to Folkestone where I am now established as a patient in the Westcliffe Hospital—my fifth hospital residence since August 8th. How much longer shall I have to be an invalid, I wonder!

December 5, 1918   Col. McKee and other specialists here are not very encouraging about being able to do much for this bad optic of mine. But its present condition is better than complete blindness, anyway; I guess I'm getting off quite lightly. I am not at all pleased to learn that I may be kept here for a week or two yet, for I never did care much for Folkestone. But being such an accomplished man of leisure, I guess I'll survive.

Last night Miller (a C.E. officer and an old school friend of McGeary) and I went to see Martin Harvey in "The Burgomaster of Stilemonde," a war play by Maeterlincke: a good play and well acted, but not really enjoyable in these peace days.

December 7, 1918   A bright, sunny day for a change! The Strait of Dover looks really beautiful from my window here, instead of sullen and forbidding as is usual in this season. Miller and I went to see "The Rapparee Trooper" at the Pleasure Gardens this afternoon and found it quite entertaining.

December 8, 1918   To Trinity Anglican Church this morning with R.J. Paterson (Lt. 22nd Bty). This afternoon I called on Sir Stephen and Lady Penfold, friends of Lt.Col. J. Keiller MacKay [formerly O.C. 6th Bde C.F.A. and a fellow patient at Buxton who later became Lieutenant-Governor of Ontario], who had asked me to pay his respects. Sir Stephen, though quite an old man, is the mayor of Folkestone and a very friendly and interesting person to meet.

December 9, 1918   A beautiful day for a sight-seeing tour! Along with friends Paterson and Miller I have taken full advantage of it by paying a visit to the historic old town of Canterbury.

Ave Mater Angliae is the motto we read on its coat of arms, and surely no place so richly deserves to be called the Mother of England! Its modern shops and streets are but a superficial cloak under which, at every turn, are evidences of a thousand and more years of history. The crowning beauty of this ancient city is, of course, its cathedral and no words can do justice to its loveliness. The old Westgate is another place of great interest: a small-scale Tower of London. St. Augustine's Abbey stands on the site of several ancient edifices dating back as far as the time of Ethelbert of Kent; and even more ancient is St. Martin's Church, where Christian services have been held regularly for at least thirteen centuries! The hotel where we had lunch and dinner (the Fleur-de-Lis Hotel) has been in business for over six centuries and many famous men <u>before us</u> have enjoyed its hospitality. But it is futile to attempt further description of a place where almost every street and every building has had so intimate a connection with important persons and events of long ago. Suffice it to say that all three of us modern pilgrims were loath to leave old Canterbury, and it was unanimously agreed that we might go far before visiting another place half so interesting and delightful.

December 10, 1918 This morning Col. McKee made a final examination of my eyes, and soon my sojourn in Folkestone will come to an end. I am advised to wear glasses for the sake of my right eye; the left one cannot be helped in this way and will never come back to normal, I'm afraid.

December 11, 1918 Was ordered back to Buxton this morning and

I caught an afternoon train which landed me at Charing Cross about 6 p.m. Fortunately, I had wired for a room at the National Hotel, else I would certainly have been badly out of luck for accommodation. London is terribly overcrowded these days, even in the middle of the week.

Barbara M. has gone home to Glasgow on account of the serious illness of her mother, so I have once again missed seeing her en route. A fellow guest at the hotel here is Phillips of the R.A.F., a Shelburne chap who was with Ewart in the 164th Bn.

December 12, 1918   Spent a very busy morning doing odd shopping and banking, and just managed to catch the 12:15 train at St. Pancras which brought me safely back to Buxton in good time for dinner. I met Dunbar (9th Bty) today in Cheapside.

December 14, 1918   Beautiful weather for Election Day! No unusual excitement here and the result seems a foregone conclusion. A letter from Glasgow this morning has brought the sad news of the death of Mrs. Macpherson: a heavy loss indeed for all our cousins there.

December 17, 1918   Am sentenced to another period of daily massage and wedge treatment, since Capt. Paterson (the M.O.) is convinced that my jaws can be opened yet a little wider. Probably a week or ten days will suffice. This afternoon was spent on an interesting visit to Haddon Hall, the former residence of the Dukes of Rutland and the House of Vernon: a fine example of a mediaeval baron's home, very commandingly situated on a hill overlooking the winding course of the Wye River. After a look through the old church in Bakewell and a stop for tea at the "Rutland Arms" we returned to Buxton by an evening train. On the way, to our surprise, our train stalled outside Miller's Dale and had to wait for an extra engine to haul us up the grade. Such stoppages seldom occur on English railroads, where trains almost invariably run right on time.

December 20, 1918   Considerable snow fell yesterday and today, but the weather is just a little too mild for it to remain on the ground. Am anticipating spending a quiet and rather lonely Christmas here in Buxton. How terribly different a Christmas from that we had all hoped for!

December 24, 1918   Major Tees marked me for "invaliding to Canada" this afternoon, so I should be home before the end of January. Shall have to be properly "boarded;" then, after perhaps a two-weeks' leave, it will be merely a case of waiting for the next sailing.

December 25, 1918   A bright Christmas Day, with frost and snow to add a home-like effect. The day has passed more happily than I had anticipated, chiefly because I have been kept occupied by the various festivities organized by the hospital and have been able to avoid much thought of other and sadder things. A very enjoyable Christmas dinner at noon was followed by a special performance of the pantomime "Cinderella" at the Opera House. And after supper the officer patients entertained the medical staff and the nurses at the "Palace." I hope my home folk have also managed to spend the day unclouded by too many sorrowful thoughts. How I wish I could have been with them!

December 26, 1918   Boxing Day is a general holiday throughout England and rather more given over to merry-making than Christmas Day itself. Today has been even brighter and frostier than yesterday and every favourable hillside had its quota of youthful enthusiasts using every conceivable type of sleigh. Lt. Seath (who was with me on course at Witley) and I went for a long tramp this afternoon, in the course of which we twice persuaded a group of schoolboys with a bob-sleigh to accept us as additional passengers on a fast trip down a long hill.

Numerous parcels have come to hand from various friends at home, but few letters during the past several days.

December 27, 1918   Attended a very enjoyable dance given by Capt. Paterson in the gymnasium. Heavy rain has carried away all the snow and the weather is now quite mild. Letter from home, dated December 6th.

December 30, 1918   An application for a two-weeks' leave was granted today. But this afternoon I was informed by the major in charge of the medical board that I shall have to be dealt with at Matlock Bath again instead of being sent home from here. This reversal of Maj. Tees's decision of last Tuesday will rather upset my plans and I cannot hope now to be home as soon as I had expected.

December 31, 1918   Today I learned from Capt. MacDonald

(M.O.) that my fate is still unsettled, since Maj. Tees and Capt. Galley are taking exception to the other doctor's ruling on my case. Shall be content to let them fight it out amongst themselves, but hope the final verdict may still spare me the inconvenience and "red tape" of Matlock Bath and the Reserve Depot. Would like to relieve the suspense of my home folk as to the time of my home-coming.

Met Johnson and White of the 23rd Bty, also George Cheney of Orangeville.

January 2, 1919   The New Year has begun very quietly here. Yesterday was a Bank Holiday; otherwise little public attention was paid to the day. The weather has been clear with some frost. Today I walked out to Grinlow Tower, otherwise known as Solomon's Temple, from which a splendid view is obtained of Buxton and the surrounding country. Col. Hutchinson, an M.O. from Argyle House, recommends my being sent home from here; so perhaps I shall have my own wish in the matter after all. Went up to "Northwood" for tea this evening.

January 4, 1919   A very heavy overnight snowfall has left a great white carpet on the ground and the trees are beautifully decorated. But one listens in vain for the merry jingle of sleigh-bells.

The daily treatment of my face and jaw has been discontinued since the end of the old year. I have now $1\frac{1}{2}''$ clearance between the teeth: not quite normal, as I find when trying to eat an apple, but much better than a quarter inch or less! I have really no longer any right to be a hospital inmate, unless I am to wait here for my sailing.

January 6, 1919   Boarded "invalided to Canada" this afternoon by Lt.Col. MacKay, Chairman of the Board [not Keiller MacKay], and may now proceed on my deferred leave while awaiting transportation home. Telegraph and telephone wires are still down as a result of the snowstorm, so I have had to <u>write</u> the Glasgow people to announce my pending arrival.

January 8, 1919   The 8:13 train from Buxton this morning gave me plenty of time to connect with the 9:40 from Victoria Station, Manchester. The northwards via Bolton, Preston and Carlyle to Glasgow Central, arriving at 5:17 p.m. Mary and John met me there, the latter having arrived home on special leave just yesterday. All are well at 53 Dixon Ave., but the mother of the family is greatly missed and the house is not the same without her.

January 9, 1919   This afternoon John and I visited the Glasgow Art Gallery and Museum, out near the university. It is a fine big building and contains a fine collection of paintings and sculpture in addition to an extensive display of antiquities, war relics and industrial exhibits.

January 10, 1919   An interesting day, spent largely in visits to two schools out in Langside. The Battlefield School (so named because it stands on ground over which the Battle of Langside was fought in 1568, resulting in the flight of Mary

Queen of Scots to England) is an elementary school, well equipped and quite similar to the newer public schools in Toronto. The Queen's Park School, which Mary M. attends, is both elementary and secondary, the work in the higher grades corresponding closely to the high school curriculum in Ontario. The art work is evidently of a very high standard in all grades; science laboratories and Manual Training and domestic science departments are quite impressive. A "housewifery" department at Battlefield School is especially noteworthy.

Peter Macpherson came home from Dunbar on a week-end leave, so I have met him now for the first time. He is quite a fine chap, well informed and very interesting to talk with. Archie is the only member of the family I have not seen and shall not see now.

Mary and John and I spent the evening with some hospitable neighbours, the MacIntoshes.

January 11, 1919 Taking a chance on the weather, Peter and John and I set out by an early train from Queen Street Station for Loch Lomond, arriving at Balloch about 10 o'clock. Boarding a little steamer there (the *Princess Patricia*), we sailed up the entire 20-mile length of the Loch to Ardlui at its northern end, calling en route at Balmaha, Luss, Rowardenen, Tarbet and Inversnaid. The boat stopped long enough at Ardui to allow us to have a good midday meal at the hotel, after which we returned southwards by the same route, reaching Balloch again at 4:20. The day was not very bright and the higher reaches of Ben Lomond and Ben

Vorlich, and even of some of the smaller hills on either side, were hidden in the mist. Most of the hilltops were snow-capped, which seemed to lend an added dignity and height to their rugged beauty. Innumerable streams flow down the steep hillsides to the Loch in thin silver cascades, with here and there a larger waterfall. Even in its sombre winter dress the Loch, with its winding course and its many little islands, is wonderfully beautiful. One feels immeasurably richer for having seen so delightful and world-famed a part of the Scottish Highlands. I am only sorry that we could not have gone on through Loch Katrine and the Trossachs. We arrived back in Glasgow about 6 o'clock, and I spent another pleasant evening with these hospitable and entertaining cousins of ours.

January 12, 1919   A quiet morning by the fireside, an enjoyable tramp through Rouken Glen with John in the afternoon, and evening church service with John and Mary and their father: these were the highlights of another winter day in Glasgow. I saw Alistair (the youngest of the brothers) for a little while, but his interests evidently lie elsewhere than at 53 Dixon Avenue.

January 13, 1919   Peter and John and I visited Glasgow Cathedral today: an interesting old building but not comparable to Canterbury and other more famous cathedrals. John and I later visited the "mystery ship" H.M.S. *Hyderabad*, which is on public exhibition here this week. This ship has disposed of at least seven (and probably several more) German U-boats, and it is interesting to examine the ingenious way in which guns and other armament were concealed on a seemingly harmless merchant vessel. In this way the British Navy lured many unsuspecting pirate subs to their doom.

January 14, 1919   An early train this morning landed Peter and John and me in Edinburgh before 10 o'clock. Peter left for Dunbar from Waverley Station shortly afterwards. John and I went over to the Registrar General's office, where I succeeded in obtaining birth certificates for Father and Uncle Angus and Aunt Kate. After lunch we boarded a motor-bus for Queens ferry to see the famous Firth of Forth bridge. A visit to the Royal Institute gave us an opportunity to see a splendid exhibit of naval photographs in colour. Darkness fell early, but after dinner we had a pleasant and interesting walk along Princes Street and around Carlton Hill. The hotels are all crowded, so John is staying for the night at a Y.M.C.A. and I am at an Officers' Club on Grosvenor Cr.

January 15, 1919   A beautiful sunny day. We got off to rather a late start on our day's programme of sightseeing, but by good management succeeded in visiting most of the places of outstanding interest before the daylight failed us. After taking in the wonderful view obtained from the towering height of Scott's Monument, we went on to the National Gallery and spent well over an hour among the pictures there. After lunch we walked up to the Old Town and visited the Castle, St. Giles Cathedral, and Holyrood Palace. High Street (the main thoroughfare of Old Edinburgh) is lined with a long row of ancient and squalid buildings, with a "close" or "wynd" leading through at intervals into unattractive courtyards. Out of many of the upper windows of these slums the day's washing hangs out to dry. The people on the street are in marked contrast to the well-dressed, prosperous-looking men and women who throng Princes Street at all hours of the day. But many of these old buildings have close associations with the history of Scotland; John Knox's house, the Canongate Tollbooth and others are of special interest. Time did not permit of carrying our explorations farther afield, and we had to make speed from Holyrood to reach the Caledonian Station in time for a 4:45 train back to Glasgow. Arrived Central Station at 6 p.m. This morning we met Jimmie Dawson (of Orangeville) on Princes St.; later on we also encountered Verrall Dedrick near the Art Gallery. It's a small world!

January 17, 1919   John left for London on his way back to Belgium by the 8:55 train from St. Enoch Station this morning. Mary and I saw him off, then walked over to Buchanan St. Stn. to catch a 9:45 train for Stirling. Arriving there at 10:30, we proceeded to a point on Borestone Brae (marked by a flagstaff, about 1½ miles from the centre of town) from which we overlooked the field of the Battle of Bannockburn. A very loquacious guide was there to give us in great detail the story of the battle. Returning to one of the hotels on King Street for lunch, we then made our way up to the castle. From the ancient ramparts of the "Key to the Highlands" a wonderful view is obtained over the surrounding country in all directions, and in the bright sunshine the snow-capped tops of Ben Lomond and other famous peaks of the Grampians stood out clearly in the far distance.

Down through the level plain between the guardian hills on either side flows the River Forth with its curious twists and turnings somewhat resembling a huge silver snake. The castle is garrisoned by a detachment of the Argyll and Sutherland Highlanders (Peter's regiment) and most of the old buildings within the castle have been transformed into modern barracks. The Douglas room is the only part now open to visitors; the old Parliament Buildings, the Palace and the Chapel Royal (none of which we were allowed to enter) probably remain much as in the olden times. Leaving the castle, we went down again into the town, taking in on our way the old High Church, the Guildhall, Mar's Work, Argyll House and other places of interest.

Failing to connect with the funny old single-track horse-tram running to the Bridge Allan, we walked out past the old Stirling Bridge to Causewayland, thence up a long winding path to the Wallace Monument on the top of Abbey Craig. A further climb of some 240 steps brought us to the highest attainable part of this impressive memorial to the great Scottish hero; and even in the failing light of late afternoon the view obtained fully justified the energy expended. As from the castle, here also river, mountain and plain stand out in a great far-reaching panorama. Earlier in the day, we were told, we could have seen the Pentland Hills far to the south and even glimpsed the great girders of the Firth of Forth bridge at Edinburgh and the top of Arthur's Seat beyond it. To the west we had a glorious view of the setting sun, while the wide plain below us gradually fell into the shadow of approaching night. Several large rooms in the monument contain interesting historical relics, including the huge sword of Wallace and other weapons and armour. After a pleasant cup of tea in the lower room we turned our steps again towards Stirling and arrived at the station in good time for the 5:30 train back to Glasgow.

January 21, 1919   Yesterday, another sight-seeing expedition with Mary: Technical School, Mitchell Library, St. Andrew's Hall, Municipal Buildings, etc. Today, back to Buxton, arriving 7:25 p.m. No definite word of sailing but it should come soon.

January 23, 1919   Caught the 9:40 train for London this morning and put up at the National Hotel upon arrival in the "Big Smoke." Had dinner with Barbara at Euston and then we visited the Gill family together out in Camden Square (No. 12 North Villas). Fine, frosty weather.

January 24, 1919   Went through Westminster Abbey this morning with Clarke (of the 2nd D.A.C.), whom I ran across in Whitehall. A beautiful building and very interesting but altogether too full of tombs and memorials, many of them erected to the memory of people who have really no place in the history of their country though they probably wielded some influence in their own day. Clarke and I then had lunch together at the Canadian Officers' Club, 8 Chesterfield Gardens, where he is staying while engaged in writing up the D.A.C. records. Lt. Sargent is representing the 5th Bde C.F.A. on the same job. In the afternoon I paid a visit to an exhibit of Canadian war memorial paintings at the Royal Academy, Burlington House, Piccadilly W. In one of the rooms there the centre of interest is the battered remains of Major Barker's Snipe in which he fought 60 Hun planes and won his V.C. After dinner Barbara and I went to see "The Man from Toronto" at the Duke of York Theatre: a rather entertaining comedy, played by the Hoey-Tully combination.

January 25, 1919   Visited the Houses of Parliament this morning: a really magnificent building, both outside and inside. The House of Lords is the most gorgeous chamber I have ever been in; the Commons is more sombre and business-like in appearance but also very beautiful. I would certainly like to have been able to attend one of the sittings of the House. Walked back to Whitehall, along Downing Street (where stands the famous but unprepossessing No. 10, the home of the Prime Minister), past a row of captured Hun aeroplanes and guns in the Mall and thence to the Grafton Galleries to see the Canadian War photographs, a fine selection of realistic war scenes beautifully coloured. A hurried visit to the National Gallery after lunch was well worth while. Proceeding eastwards by underground to St. Paul's Cathedral, I found an afternoon service just commencing so could not make much of a tour of the interior. Decided to return to Buxton this evening, so caught the fast Midland Express at St. Pancras and reached my destination at 10:35.

January 29, 1919   There are persistent rumours today of a sailing on or before next Tuesday. Hope they are right!

February 1, 1919　Final orders received to sail tomorrow with a
party of some 50 or 60 other officers from here, leaving
Buxton at noon. Rather anxious about Ewart, having
received no word from him since January 4th.

LIVERPOOL TO PORTLAND, MAINE

February 2, 1919　Leaving Buxton at one p.m., after a hearty send-
off by the officers and nurses still remaining there, a two-
hour run brought us to Liverpool, where we immediately
embarked on the hospital ship *Araguaya*. Soon after six
o'clock we put out into midstream, where we shall probably lie overnight. This is evidently quite a comfortable ship
but it is not likely to make the crossing in much under ten
days. We have a jolly crew aboard and are all anticipating a
pleasant voyage, weather permitting. Farewell selections
were played by a Liverpool band as we pulled away from
the dock.

February 3, 1919　Getting under way about 8 o'clock this morning, we steamed slowly down the river and dropped our
pilot two hours later. Our course lies around the south of
Ireland and across to Portland, Maine, according to all
available information. Very smooth going so far. One of my
bed-fellows is Lt. Smith of No. 4 Co., 16th Btn. Lt. Frame
(M.M.G.) is also located nearby.

February 4, 1919　Second day out. We cleared the coast of Ireland
this morning and appear to be sailing somewhat south of due
west. Not much of a sea, but this old tub rolls considerably

and most of us have been feeling none too comfortable at times. I have managed to retain quite a good appetite however, and the meals are very good. Some rain squalls during the day. We have passed safely through "The Devil's Hole."

February 5, 1919   A beautiful sunny day, quite mild but with a fresh bracing breeze blowing from the southwest. Deck games helped to pass the daylight hours pleasantly and a quiet rubber of bridge with Paton, Frame and Smith whiled away the time until we were sleepy enough for bed. Am reading Parker's *Battle of the Strong* and find it very entertaining.

February 6, 1919   Fourth day out and our fine weather still holds. No need for overcoats as yet. The ship is pitching considerably but everyone seems to have found his "sea legs." During the first two days we carried lifebelts up on deck and a "P.V." (Paravane) was towed along on either side of the ship. Yesterday and today, however, both of these precautionary measures against floating mines have been discontinued.

February 7, 1919   Today we have run through occasional rain squalls; otherwise fair weather still makes pleasant the lengthening daylight hours. Among those on board I have discovered Robertson, formerly 67th Bty, now minus one leg. Again I realize how lucky I have been!

February 8, 1919   The wind has become noticeably colder, but the sun still shines brightly and most of us are thoroughly enjoying the voyage. Few are troubled now with anything approaching seasickness.

February 9, 1919   The distance now covered totals 1850 miles. Tuesday night should find us nearing our destination and I should be home by Thursday or Friday. Church service this morning was conducted by Capt. Pringle, the ship's chaplain. The weather is still clear but increasingly cold.

February 10, 1919   A peculiar spell of mild weather during the night and early morning gave way again before a piercing west wind. The decks are too wet with rain and spray to permit of outdoor games and the day has passed largely in walking, reading and bridge. The crew put on a concert in one of the lower messes tonight before a capacity audience.

February 11, 1919   The sea became considerably rougher overnight and sleet has fallen at intervals during the day. Rather hard to keep the dishes in their proper places at meals. Only 270 miles were covered during the past twenty-four hours.

February 12, 1919   Clear sunshine today but very cold outdoors. The sea has become less rough and we seem to be making fair speed; but this is the tenth day out and we are becoming weary of so slow a homeward voyage. Tonight there is moonlight and a relatively calm sea. Almost sorry to go to bed.

February 13, 1919   Eleventh day out—and last! We sighted land during the morning and docked at Portland about 3 p.m. A rousing reception awaited us, and for the rest of the day various groups representing the mayor and people of the city moved about the docks and the ship distributing comforts of all kinds and radiating good cheer and hospitality. The city band enlivened the proceedings with patriotic and rag-time airs. At night I went ashore for an hour or two and walked through the main business section of the city. The bright cluster lights and the electric signs were almost startling after the wartime darkness of English and French cities.

Paton left about 9 p.m. for P.E.I. and Smith and Frame by a western train later on, so our genial little company is already breaking up. The rest of us expect to leave tomorrow and I should reach Toronto by Saturday.

February 14, 1919 Went for another interesting walk up town this morning, but the time hung very heavily on our hands until we finally entrained and pulled out for Montreal about 4:30 p.m. All on board are for Toronto and vicinity and we hope for a fast run. Considerable snow is falling as we proceed.

February 15, 1919 Slept fairly comfortably until about half-past six this morning, when we found ourselves at a junction point just outside Montreal. After some delay we got under way again but made discouragingly slow progress, stopping at several stations en route, and did not reach North Toronto Station until 8 o'clock at night. There a great crowd had assembled to meet us and among them I soon located Father and Mother and a number of Toronto cousins. George Garton took us all down to Rose Avenue for a very happy celebration lasting well into the night. Mother went home with Aunt Annie (Avison) but Father is staying here at "93" with me. Had a chat with Arthur over the 'phone and sent Angus a wire. It is a wonderfully happy feeling to be with "my ain folk" again.

February 16, 1919   We got off to a late start this morning, Father and I, but managed to reach Margueretta St. in time for lunch with Aunt Annie, Uncle John, Mother and Frank Perchard. Wilfred and Ella Avison dropped in for a few minutes, after which I accompanied Father and Mother down to Geoff St. (147 and 92) and called also at 52 Fermanagh Ave. to see Annie and Matt Irving. From there we proceeded to the Creeds for tea and I walked over to Close Ave. for a few minutes to see John and Mrs. Biggart. Tom Huston called to see me at Spencer Ave., having missed me at the station last night. Bert Creed then took us over to the hospital to see Carrie, whom we found looking fairly well after her operation. Returning with Father and Mother to George's, I set out again (at a disgracefully late hour) for 34 Rosemount Ave. and spent a very happy evening with Carrie MacFayden.

February 17, 1919   The 8:10 train from North Toronto Station carried Father and Mother and me, all too slowly, on the final stage of my homeward journey, landing us in Orangeville some time after ten. At the station a great crowd of old friends made me welcome and escorted me home. Arthur is looking well and fit, as big as I am now. Yesterday and today have passed as in a dream and I am kept wondering if I shall not soon wake up and find myself back in France or in Buxton Hospital. Many good friends have called to see me during the afternoon and evening.

February 18, 1919   My dream still continues but is beginning now to become more convincing and realistic. Made several calls with Mother this afternoon.

February 19, 1919   Attended a Literary Society meeting at the high school with Bun Aiken this afternoon. Quite like old times, but the familiar faces of former years are sadly missing—except Miss Strang and Mary Gabriel. Bright, frosty weather has continued ever since my return home and I am gradually becoming convinced that my dream is really true.

February 21, 1919   The Orangeville branch of the G.W.V.A. (Great War Veterans' Ass'n) was organized tonight. Col. Preston was made President, Mr. Firth Sec'y Treas. and Bun Aiken 2/V.P.

February 23, 1919   Church services, morning and evening; Mr. Morris preaching. Tea with Col. And Mrs. Preston.

February 24, 1919   Mrs. McIntyre came down from Grand Valley this morning for a little visit; also Uncle Archie and Aunt McGill from Erin.

February 27, 1919   To Toronto with Arthur by this morning's train. A delightful afternoon with old friends at Annette Street School. Supper with Effie, Ella and Sarah McGill at 203 Pacific Ave. To Aunt Annie's for the night, by way of Rosemount Ave.

February 28, 1919   A day filled with shopping and much visiting. Art and I had lunch with Mrs. Robertson at Simpson's. During the afternoon I called to see my faithful little correspondent, ex-pupil and "niece" Patsy Washington; also ran across (in Eaton's) another ex-pupil, Marjorie Mahoney, and "Pad" Lewis (now in 1st Year Med.) Had dinner with

George and Kate and returned to Margueretta St. while Art went to see a show.

March 1, 1919 March made an effort to come in "like a lion" but it has not been completely successful and our visiting continued to progress well. After a noon dinner with the Fergusons, Will accompanied us over the new viaduct to Lyall Ave. in the Far East, where we had a delightful visit with the Prices. Renewed acquaintance after several years with Mary, Dorothy, Marjorie and Gordon; Gladys was not at home. Returning to the West End, we had supper with Wilfred and Ella Avison on Indian Road; then back to Margueretta St.

March 2, 1919 Frank Perchard and Art went with me to Victoria Church for the morning service. Very kindly received by many old friends there. Art stayed for dinner at Cyril Carson's (High Park Ave.) but later in the afternoon we both called to see the Creeds and remained for supper and the evening church service at Cowan Ave. church.

March 3, 1919 Art left for home on the morning train and I caught the 8:29 (C.P.R.) at Sunnyside Station for Hamilton. From there a radial car took me to the Brant Military Hospital at Burlington. The officer patients here are very comfortably quartered in summer cottages overlooking the lake. Garfield Gordon is here, also Lt. Douglas (P.P.C.L.I.) whom I knew at F.O.E. in 1914-15. Many of the officers who were with me on the *Araguaya* have also reported here today.

March 4, 1919   Garfield and I went into Hamilton this morning for examination by Lt.Col. Osborne, the eye specialist. His report on my "optic" after a very thorough examination tallies closely with that of Col. McKee at Folkestone and, since the damage cannot be corrected, my stay here should not be prolonged beyond the end of this week. Am rather expecting to be boarded about Friday.

March 6, 1919   On a sudden happy inspiration this morning I went into Hamilton and caught the 10:20 radial for Brantford, arriving there an hour later. Found everybody at home at 135 Brant Ave. including Duncan, who had arrived from overseas just last night, and spent a most enjoyable day. All these Fitzpatrick cousins (except Duncan) have grown almost beyond recognition in the eight or nine years since I last saw them, but they are the same merry family as of yore and it has been a rare treat to spend these few hours with them. A 9:05 car from Brantford gave me a good connection at Hamilton and I was back in hospital before 11 p.m.

March 7, 1919   Went up before a medical board this afternoon and am now recommended for discharge. But my papers have to be submitted to the authorities in Toronto for approval before I can be released from here; in the meantime I have managed to obtain a weekend leave. A 7:35 train from Hamilton landed me in Guelph at 9:15 p.m. Marjorie Richardson and Bessie McLaren, who is with Marjorie in the "Wyndham Inn" enterprise, met me at the station. Gordon McLaren is also visiting with the Richardsons.

March 8, 1919   Paid an interesting visit today with Gordon to the O.A.C. Met Cameron St. John, formerly 67th Bty, who is now a student there.

March 9, 1919   Morning church service with Harry Richardson, an afternoon of music at the house, and a pleasant evening visit with the Harvey family, cousins of the Richardsons. But how my heart aches for poor Marjorie that it is not Ross instead of me who has returned! It is hard to overcome the bitter regrets that still rise so often in the mind.

March 10, 1919   A 3:10 train from Guelph and a 5:10 Burlington car returned me to the hospital by 6 p.m. Several of the officers who were boarded with me on Friday left this afternoon, but I cannot yet find out just when I am due to go.

March 11, 1919   To Hamilton early this afternoon. Located Charlie Brown at the Bell Telephone Co. offices and through him met a Miss Jean Murdoch (an acquaintance of Ewart's and Duncan Fitzpatrick's) and a Miss Fraser, whose sister is married to Ted Johnston, brother of Kate Garton. Later looked up Harry Reid but missed Mr. Bell and the Rohmer boys. Stayed for dinner at the Royal Connaught Hotel and returned to the hospital by the 8:10 car.

March 12, 1919　A pleasant little party was given by the nurses this evening. Met a Miss Kyles, among others, a niece of Dr. Kyles and now on duty here.

March 13, 1919　Had dinner with Charlie Brown at the Wentworth Arms this evening and looked up Albert Rohmer before returning to hospital by the 8:10 car.

March 14, 1919　Paton arrived at Brant House from P.E.I. last night and I feel rather sorry to have had to leave today. Caught the 11:45 from Burlington, arriving Toronto 1 p.m. Lunched at the King Edward Hotel with Dalgleish and Doc. Binkley. Reported to #1 Queen's Park and received discharge, effective March 22, after exactly 2 years and 8 months in the army. Also called at 40 Richmond St. West to straighten out matters re pay. Went home with George Garton for supper and remained there overnight.

March 15, 1919　Lunched with Alan Cuthbertson at the Board of Trade (top of Royal Bank) and spent the afternoon and evening with Carrie M. at 34 Rosemount.

March 16, 1919　Attended morning service at St. Enoch's Church with George and Kate. Met Forbes (164th Bn) and Herb Davis there. Went to 147 Geoffrey St. for supper and called at the Creeds' on the way back to Rose Ave.

March 17, 1919　My 24th birthday was celebrated with beaucoup rain. I interviewed Dr. Vogt at the Conservatory re Angus's song ("In Flanders Fields"). Lunched with George and Mr. Deacon. Had a talk with Mr. Wilson (principal) at Annette

St. School this afternoon, then called to see the Mahoneys on High Park Ave. and stayed there for supper. Took in a bright little comedy ("Leave it to Jane") at the Royal Alex tonight with Carrrie M. A very enjoyable evening!

March 18, 1919   Had a chat with Dr. Carson this morning. Visited Mrs. Steele and the Bedfords during the afternoon and spent the evening with the Creeds, who kindly agreed to overlook my alleged neglect of them during the past three days.

Mar 19, 1919   Had lunch with George G., then proceeded to the Orthopaedic Hospital on Christie St. where I located Fred Patterson, whom I had last seen in Buxton. A couple of hours with Carrie M. brought me to train time and I reached home at 7:30 p.m. Father and Mother met me at the station.

March 21, 1919   An "expedition" to the bottom of my trunk today brought forth the wherewithal to dress in civvies, in which I made my debut once again as a peaceful citizen at a dance at O.M.S. A very enjoyable affair, attended by many former students whose presence served to offset the effect of the unfamiliar faces of present-day pupils.

March 22, 1919   Last day in khaki. My discharge takes effect from today. (Authority 2MD, 30-M-357, dated 28.3.19)

EPILOGUE

It is evident that my Diary was, largely, a means of escape from the war and not an attempt to portray war in all its stark reality. Sanity and peace of mind could be preserved only by thinking and talking and writing about the more normal things of life: family and friends; the beauty of the unravaged French countryside behind the battle lines, the fascinating interest of Old England and Scotland and the heroic spirit of their people; the hoped-for homecoming at war's end.

The overall length of my story surprises me, now that I have typed it out in a more readable form. Much of it was written, during my year as a signaller in the 9th Battery, in "the long night watches;" for, even during comparatively quiet intervals between engagements with the enemy, communication lines had to be kept open and night duty was a common occurrence for each one of us. Lengthy entries were made, also, during periods of rest at the Wagon Lines where duties were light and time hung heavily on our hands. In times of intense activity in forward areas, needless to say, entries (if any) could be made only sketchily and on scrap paper, to be copied later into the permanent record. But the habit of keeping a diary, once established, continued throughout my entire period of service in the C.E.F.

It has been a thrilling experience to recall the comradeship of those years and the light-hearted way in which men together faced indescribable hardships and dangers. The sacrifices they made were the measure of their devotion to a great cause, and hopes ran high that by their efforts on the field of battle Canada and the world would be saved for a richer and better destiny in the years to come.

It must never be said that their sacrifices were in vain. No sacrifice, willingly made for others, can but make the world a better place to live in. If their hopes for a permanent peace were destined to remain yet awhile unrealized, the responsibility must lie squarely on the shoulders of those who survived the holocaust and proved unequal to the task of leading the world into the millennium. Even a second World War, with its one million Canadians under arms and its forty thousand dead, did not bring peace; but progress *is* being made and the nations of the world, by the grace of God, will one day forego for all time the use of armed might to settle their differences. Until that blessed time comes, the soldier, sailor, and airman must continue to guard our beloved country against the loss of liberty and freedom so dearly won throughout the years on fields of battle.

June 30, 1965.

GLOSSARY

B.C. Party	The Battery Commander's Party (The signallers whose duty it was to maintain all necessary communications lines for the battery.
Bde.	Brigade (of artillery or of infantry)—4 Batteries or 4 Battalions. <u>Examples</u>: The 3rd Bde. C.F.A. was made up of the 9th, 10th, 11th and 12th Batteries. The 7th Infantry Bde. was made up of the P.P.C.L.I., the Royal Canadian Regiment, and the 42nd and 49th Battalions.
Blighty	An affectionate nickname for England; hence applied to a wound which resulted in a man being sent back to England.
Bn.	Battalion (of artillery or of infantry)
Bty.	Battery (of artillery)
C.E.F.	Canadian Expeditionary Force
C.F.A.	Canadian Field Artillery
Co.	Company (of infantry)
Corps.	The Canadian Corps consisted of all troops of the 1st, 2nd, 3rd and the 4th Divisions and (in the final year of war), a 5th Div. of Field Artillery.
D.A.C.	Divisional Ammunition Column: an artillery depot, one for each of the four divisions, through which ammunition and supplies and reinforcements were routed to all the forward areas.
Div.	Division—Four Brigades of infantry, four Brigades of field artillery and all supporting troops including heavy artillery.
F.O.P	Forward Observation Post: an O.P. in advance of the guns.
G.S. Wagon	General Service Wagon, for distribution of supplies.
HQ	Headquarters of a Bty., Bn., Bde., Div., Corps, etc.
Limber	The detachable front of a gun-carriage.
L.O.	Liaison Officer, accompanied by signallers, whose duty it was to maintain communications between infantry and artillery. During an attack the Liaison Party went forward with the infantry to report back the progress of the attacking troops.
O.C. or C.O.	Officer Commanding
O.P.	Observation Post: a point of vantage from which enemy positions and movements and the results of our own gunfire might be observed.
Pill Box	A round-shaped concrete strong-point on the Ypres front.
R.F.A.	Royal Field Artillery
R.F.C.	Royal Flying Corps (later to become R.A.F., Royal Air Force)
W.L.	Wagon Lines.

OUTLINE OF ARMY TRAINING AND ACTIVE WAR SERVICE

1914-1915

September to May: In training with C.O.T.C. (Canadian Officers' Training Corps) at University of Toronto while attending the Faculty of Education, with rank of sergeant. Qualified for Lieutenancy in the Infantry of the Active Militia. (Cert. #33491. Dated Aug.5, 1915.)

1915-1916

September to June: Taught for one school year at Annette Street Public School. Operation in March in preparation for enlistment.

1916

July 14: Enlisted as a gunner in the 67th (Varsity) Battery, Canadian Field Artillery, Toronto. Battery moved to Niagara-on-the-Lake Aug. 4, and to Petawawa Aug. 25-26. Assigned to a course in Signalling.

October 21: Left Petawawa by train for Halifax with No. 4 Draft from Bty.

October 24: Boarded H.M.T. Grampian in Halifax Harbour.

October 26: Sailed from Halifax for England.

November 5: Arrived in Liverpool and proceeded by train to Shorncliffe Camp, near Folkestone. Assigned again to Signalling, at Risboro' Barracks.

1917

January 19-20: To France, Southampton to Le Havre. To 1st D.A.C. at Barlin (Jan. 25) and to 9th Bty C.F.A. at Hersin (Feb. 13).

April 9: Beginning of the Battle of Vimy Ridge (Apr. 9-14).

August 15: Beginning of the Battle of Hill 70 (Aug. 15-25).

October 12-15: North to Ypres in Belgium.

October 26: Beginning of the Battle of Passchendaele (October 26-November 10).

October 29: The Macphersons acquire a D.S.O. [Ross] and an M.M. [Donald] on two different parts of the battle front.

November 13-17: Back to the Vimy front.

December 16-17: To England via Boulogne and Folkestone for Cadet Course leading to Commission, Witley Camp.

1918

January 1: New Years' Eve and New Years' Day spent in London with Ross and Doug and Ewart and Uncle Arthur Willson.

May 17:	Completed course for commissioned rank of Lieutenant. (Cert. #32259, dated May 23, 1918.)
June 1:	Returned to France via Folkestone and Boulogne.
June 2:	To Etaples (Base Depot).
June 11:	To Calonne Ricourt (Canadian Corps Reserve Camp).
June 12:	To Aubigny, overnight, then to Monchiet (2nd D.A.C.).
July 31-August 4:	South, by secret night marches, to the Amiens front.
August 8:	Beginning of the Battle of Amiens (Aug. 8-11). Wounded east of Cachy. Taken by stretcher to a field dressing station at Cachy, then by ambulance to the railhead and by train to Rouen (Aug. 9).
August 23-24:	To England on the hospital ship Essequibo, via Le Havre and Southampton. To Prince of Wales Hospital in London (formerly the Great Central Hotel). R.560.
September 5:	Deeply shocked by news, brought to me by Ewart, of Ross's death in action on August 26th.
October 8:	To Canadian Convalescent Hospital at Matlock Bath, Derby.
October 17:	To Buxton, Granville Canadian Special Hospital (formerly the Palace Hotel), R.45.
October 28:	News received of Doug's M.C., awarded for action in the Battle of Amiens, August 1918.
November 11:	Armistice Day. In Buxton.
November 29:	To Westcliffe Hospital, Folkestone, for eye examination.
December 11:	Returned to Buxton, Derbyshire. Overnight in London.

1919

February 2:	Sailed for Liverpool on the hospital ship Araguaya.
February 13:	Arrived in Portland, Maine.
February 15:	Arrived in Toronto. Met by Father and Mother and cousins.
February 17:	Arrived home in Orangeville.
March 3:	To Brant Military Hospital, Burlington (formerly the Brant Inn).
March 14:	Returned to Toronto and to Orangeville (Mar. 19).
March 22:	Last day in khaki.